Adventures in ODYSSEY

RADIO SCRIPTS, VOL. 3

FOCUS ON THE FAMILY

Adventures in ODYSSEY

RADIO SCRIPTS, VOL. 3

by Paul McCusker

Lillenas PUBLISHING COMPANY

KANSAS CITY, MO 64141

CONTENTS

Before You Take Off for Odyssey

by Paul McCusker

On behalf of the entire *Adventures in Odyssey* production team, I'm pleased to welcome you to the long-awaited *Adventures in Odyssey* script publishing series. I say "long-awaited" because, for as long as *Adventures in Odyssey* has been produced as a half-hour radio drama, listeners have been after Focus on the Family to release many of the radio scripts for use in their churches, youth groups, Bible schools, Sunday Schools, education, and puppet programs. We're pleased to finally be able to do that, thanks in no small part to Lillenas Publishing Company's remarkable drama outreach.

The plays enclosed in this volume are the original radio scripts, each the equivalent of a "one-act" play. You'll see the original notes to establish the characters, settings, and sound-effects for radio. We're now including some extra production notes to help you with your own "live" presentation. We're purposefully keeping the notes sparse, though, because we've learned over the years that each venue for performance will be unique, with its own specific needs and demands. We can't anticipate them all. As always, flexibility and creativity will make all the difference in how these scripts can be adapted for the stage. And you can't go wrong getting ideas by listening to the original radio production, available from Focus on the Family.

We're also including the original concluding comments from Chris, the host of *Adventures in Odyssey*. These comments may help you with any remarks you may want to make at the end of your presentation.

Adventures in Odyssey has been around for over a decade, and through the radio broadcasts and cassette releases, the scripts you have here are thoroughly "tested." We're confident that your own presentation of the *Odyssey* world will be inspirational, educational, and fun for your cast, crew, and especially your audience.

For Those Who Don't Know

You don't have to be well-versed with *Adventures in Odyssey* to make use of these scripts. They should apply to any audience anywhere. However, to help you understand the "world" of *Odyssey*, here's an introduction (adapted from the *Adventures in Odyssey* Writer's Guidelines) . . .

THE WORLD OF ODYSSEY

Imagine it. You're walking through a small American town on a bright, sunshiny day. It's the kind of day when everything is clearly in focus; the brick-reds, stone-grays, and pillar-whites of the shops along the Main Street contrast sharply with the milky pavement under your feet and the lush greens and browns of the park across the charcoal road. People smile and bid you a "good day" as they pass, even though you're a stranger to them.

Eventually you reach an odd-looking Victorian house with a sign above the door that says *Whit's End*. Inside, you find it's an old-fashioned ice cream parlor and, if you believe the sign, a "discovery emporium." You don't know what this means until you begin to wander through the many rooms. Each one is filled with wondrous displays for "hands-on" learning, games, books, a theater and cinema, a computer room, a radio broadcasting studio, and—

Wait a minute. Here's something called "The Bible Room" and there, working next to a machine that looks like a cross between a telephone booth and helicopter cockpit, you see the owner of this establishment. He's a tall, sparkly-eyed fellow with unruly white hair and bushy white mustache. He wipes his hands on a rag and steps forward to shake your hand. "Hi, I'm John Whittaker," he says. "But you can call me Whit."

Whit explains that the machine he's been working on is an invention of his called "The Imagination Station"; designed to help kids use their imaginations to bring the Bible "to life." In essence, it's a time machine that will take you back to the moment when David defeated Goliath, or Elijah brought fire down from heaven, or yes, the crucifixion and resurrection of Jesus Christ. "It's up to you, really. It can take you to any period in time you want," Whit explains.

You stand back to take it all in. The friendly town. The wondrous shop. The sparkly-eyed inventor. The time machine. It seems too good to be true. But it isn't because you *believe* you're really there. It's the start of your own Adventure . . . in Odyssey.

THE CREATION OF ODYSSEY

It began as an experiment. In 1987, Dr. James Dobson's Focus on the Family produced a family drama series. It was called *Family Portraits* and chronicled the lives and times of Odyssey residents—including John Whittaker, his family, and Whit's End.

Audience response was so favorable, Focus on the Family renamed the program *Adventures in Odyssey* and created new and exciting situations that ranged from normal family conflicts to high adventure. Its purpose was to bring scriptural principles to life through memorable characters, realistic dramas, heartfelt comedy, and even a bit of fantasy using the "theater of the mind." There are over 400 half-hour episodes produced, and it is currently heard on over 1,400 radio facilities on weekends and 800 radio facilities on weekdays throughout North America and worldwide.

Demand for *Adventures in Odyssey* resulted in the distribution of the show—made available individually and in compilation albums of 12 episodes.

SOME OF THE PEOPLE AND PLACES YOU'LL MEET IN ODYSSEY

These are just a handful of the many characters you'll encounter from adventure to adventure in Odyssey.

John Avery Whittaker, Odyssey, and "Whit's End"

John Avery Whittaker is not the type of person who stands out in a crowd. As a matter of fact, unless you get to know him really well, it might be very easy to lose him in a large group of people. Someone once said that he looks like a cross between Mark Twain and a young C. S. Lewis—a full white mustache, a rather unruly white mop of hair, and a round, pleasant face.

John Avery Whittaker—or Whit, as he is best known around town—is a writer, inventor, and entrepreneur. He's always had a love for kids and, during his stint as a junior high English teacher, felt concerned that so many of his students were suffering from the "signs of the times": broken homes, single-parent households, crumbling morals, and the pressure to grow up too fast. He wanted to do something about it.

After his own children moved on and his wife, Jenny, passed away unexpectedly, Whit bought and renovated the old Fillmore Recreation Center that sat near the center of town in McCalister Park. Part Victorian house and part modern additions, it had all the space Whit needed for his "place of adventure and discovery" for all the kids in Odyssey. He called it Whit's End and officially billed it as "an ice cream parlor and discovery emporium."

At the time Whit explained, "Whit's End is a place full of adventure and discovery, filled with books and activities, fun and games, arts and crafts, uplifting conversation, and some of the best ice cream in the state. It's a place where people can experience the excitement of learning, and build character and confidence; a place to make friends and learn how to keep relationships healthy; a place to find out what the Bible says and what God wants us to do with our lives. But most of all, Whit's End is a place where kids of all ages can just be kids."

Some of Whit's End's attractions include the state's largest hand-made electric train set (with the cars made by the patrons themselves), an "inventor's corner" (where kids are encouraged to make their ideas come to life), a small audio studio where Kid's Radio broadcasts, a Little Theater, a well-stocked library, and The Bible Room—where artifacts, museum pieces, displays, and an incredible invention called The Imagination Station help the Bible "come alive" in the imaginations of the kids. There is also the Room of Consequence, which allows kids to play out the consequences of their decisions and actions.

Tom Riley

Whit's best friend. Tom Riley is one of the most popular figures in Odyssey. A farmer by trade (and quite successful), he is now retired from that profession and spends a good deal of his time coaching Little League sports, working with the Odyssey City Council, and serving as an elder at the church Whit attends.

On the surface, Tom seems like the epitome of the "good ol' boy." Very mild mannered and easy-going in a Henry Fonda way, he has a confidence about him that seems to be born in many country folks, and this attribute often helps him arrive at simple solutions that sometimes even Whit is unable to see. Tom is good-natured with a gentle sense of humor—and absolutely no compunctions about making use of it.

Connie Kendall

An ageless teen employee at Whit's End, Connie is into modern trends, or at least as much of it as one can get in Odyssey. She is not a native Odyssean. She and her divorced mother, June, moved to Odyssey from Los Angeles. Although she became a Christian at the end of her first year on the show, Connie still has a stubborn streak that challenges conventional thinking and questions many of the assumptions Christians make.

Connie is a very comical character in many respects, but she is also an excellent vehicle through which ethics, biblical principles, and Christian living can be explained. Of particular note is Connie's very sisterly relationship with Eugene Meltsner . . .

Eugene Meltsner

An advanced college student, Eugene attends Campbell College, studying science (all kinds) and working as a teaching assistant. He approached John Whittaker for an internship on the advice of his professor—believing that working next to such an intelligent man would benefit him in his studies. Thus, he now works part time at Whit's End as an inventor and odd-jobs man. He is very straightforward in his intelligence (in almost *all* fields) and originally approached everything with an impeccable logic. He doesn't take offense easily, either, when people show a lack of interest in his vast array of knowledge (often displayed in spontaneous "lectures" to whoever is standing by).

Lucy Cunningham-Schultz

At 12-ish, Lucy is bright and sincere in her Christian beliefs. So sincere, in fact, that those beliefs often get her into lots of trouble and make her a perfect foil for the more mischievous Jack Davis.

Jack Davis

Look up the word "rascal" in the dictionary, and you'll find a picture of Jack Davis. He's good-natured, fun, but inclined to mischief and no small amount of mayhem (but never anything vindictive).

The Barclay Family

The Barclays are Christians, yet (like most families) struggle with how to implement Christian principles in their daily lives and activities.

GEORGE BARCLAY, the father, who wants to be the "spiritual" leader of the house—but sometimes fumbles the responsibility. He is a loving husband/father.

MARY BARCLAY, caring and compassionate wife/mother, who works hard to keep sanity among her husband and children.

JIMMY BARCLAY, who is a typical boy in his outlook of life and understanding of Christianity.

DONNA BARCLAY is the "older" sister and rambunctious daughter going through the typical phases of a teenager. She is prone to complain and look to "keeping up with what her friends are doing."

For even more insight into *Adventures in Odyssey* and its characters, we strongly recommend that you read *The Complete Guide to Adventures in Odyssey* by Phil Lollar (published by Focus on the Family).

How to Read These Scripts

The *Adventures in Odyssey* radio script format is a lot like the formats for television and movie screenplays. We thought it was easier for the actors to read than the traditional play format. Here's what you'll find . . .

SCENE 1
[LIKE A REGULAR PLAY, THE SETTING, SCENE DIRECTIONS, SOUND EFFECTS, MUSIC, AND CHARACTER ACTIONS ARE PLACED HERE. THEY EXPLAIN ANYTHING THAT MAY NOT BE OBVIOUS IN OTHER PARTS OF THE SCRIPT.]

CHARACTER 1:
(ANY SPECIFIC INSTRUCTIONS FOR THE CHARACTER ARE PLACED HERE. "PAUSES" AND/OR "BEATS" ARE INDICATED HERE.) Then, on with the line.

CHARACTER 2:
Like a regular play, instructions for a character may also appear in the middle of a line (THE INSTRUC-TIONS), then go back to the line.

"Pauses" are those times when a character stops speaking in order to think, feel, or otherwise break the rhythm of speech before continuing. For our purposes, a "beat" is a shorter "pause"—a break in the rhythm or flow of the character's speech in order to change the subject or introduce an entirely different tone or attitude. These will be obvious when they appear.

Don't panic about references to music. Each *Adventures in Odyssey* episode had custom music made for it, but that doesn't mean you have to. However, if you have the ability for transitional music in some form, these are the places to put them while you accomplish scene changes.

The Big Broadcast

INTRODUCTION

You may remember from volume 1 of this series that two kids named Brad and Sherman tried to start a "radio station" for the kids of Whit's End. They called it "Kid's Radio," and sadly, it failed because many of the kids who wanted to be on the radio didn't want to commit to the hard work it would take to make it a success. That episode was called, appropriately enough, *Kid's Radio.* Over a year later, the *Adventures in Odyssey* creative team decided it was time to blow the dust off the idea of a radio station for kids and relaunch it. The result was *The Big Broadcast,* which originally aired on June 9, 1990. It contains a fair amount of silliness—a game show, interruptions for "special reports," and a humorous twist on Jesus' story of the Good Samaritan.

An explanation about the version of the script you have here is in order. Often in producing *Adventures in Odyssey* the writers would create a preliminary draft of the script that would be edited down for the final recorded program. Entire scenes are often lost to accommodate the production's time constraints. Now, for the first time ever, we've restored sections of the original script that were cut out of the radio show.

PRODUCTION NOTES

Because this is a sketch-based program, you have a lot of flexibility with your production. You can do the entire script as a full-blown play or use only the sections that suit you. This can be performed in a true "live" radio drama style, with microphones, music stands, and sound effects. Or a reader's theatre approach might work better. Or you may want to mix live performance with prerecorded sections or quick bits performed from offstage. It's up to you.

The set can be a "radio station" with microphones and sound effects scattered all over. The main announcer/narrator can read from a podium off to one side. You can take dramatic "license" and set up sections of the stage to accommodate the various scenes as simply or elaborately as you want. The game show can have a podium for the host and a couple of chairs for the contestants. The interview with the coach can be two chairs set center stage. The commercial with Jimmy and Lucy can be done downstage without any props, as if they're walking "backstage." The Good Samaritan sketch can take place like any church "bathrobes" drama—all over the stage—with our sleuth using additional 20th century detective garb.

You may want to have someone off to one side of the stage with headphones and a sign to indicate when the audience should applaud (APPLAUSE) and/or laugh. Practice this with your audience before you begin—when the sign is held up, they should applaud, and so on; when it is lowered, they stop. It'll be a lot of fun for them to be included.

The first scene is optional, by the way, with the previous set covered in tarps until Whit and Tom pull them off. (If you cut the first scene, you may want to cut the very last scene as well.)

CAST OF CHARACTERS

In the original radio program of *The Big Broadcast*, we doubled-up many of the parts. You don't have to do that here—choosing instead to cast each character. Here's the full list:

JOHN AVERY WHITTAKER: *the wise and friendly "inventor" of Kid's Radio who also serves as our*

>GENERAL ANNOUNCER

>GAME SHOW ANNOUNCER

>COMMERCIAL ANNOUNCER

>NEWS REPORTER

TOM RILEY: *folksy friend of Whit who also plays as our*

>GAME SHOW HOST

>FIRST PRIEST

>LEVITE

EUGENE MELTSNER: *the "brainy" employee of Whit at Whit's End, who is also our*

>ANNOUNCER

>THE MAN IN THE STREET

>SPORTS INTERVIEWER

>SAM MARITAN, PRIVATE EYE

JIMMY BARCLAY: *a boy of around 10 or 11, who also plays*

>CONTESTANT IN THE GAME SHOW

>THE INNKEEPER

LUCY CUNNINGHAM-SCHULTZ: *a girl of around 10 or 11, who is also*

>CONTESTANT IN THE GAME SHOW

>LUCY CUTIE IN THE SAM MARITAN SKETCH

COACH FRED ZACHARY: *a not-so-bright coach in the Yogi Berra mold who also tends to use the word "whatchacall" a lot*

SCENE 1

[A SMALL ROOM IN WHIT'S END WHERE THE KID'S RADIO EQUIPMENT IS STORED. WHIT AND TOM ARE GASPING AND GROANING AS THEY MOVE A DESK INTO THE ROOM.]

TOM:

Got it? Careful now . . . watch out for the door-jamb.

WHIT:

I'm OK . . .

TOM:

Where's it go?

WHIT:

I cleared a spot in the corner . . . there . . .

TOM:

Right . . . got it . . . this OK?

WHIT:

Fine. Let's set it down.

[THEY PUT THE DESK DOWN.]

TOM:

(GASPING) Whoo-ee. Next time you want to put furniture in storage, make it a chair or a paperweight. This desk of yours was *heavy*.

WHIT:

(BREATHLESS) Maybe I should've emptied the drawers first.

TOM:

What?

WHIT:

Just kidding. I'm thinking of donating it to the church—for the pastor. I figured this was a good place to store it until I do.

TOM:

Yeah—I haven't been in this room for a long time. What's under all these tarps—more furniture?

WHIT:

(CHUCKLES) Take a look for yourself.

TOM:

(THROWS THE TARP OFF) Good grief, is that the old radio equipment you pulled out of the basement?

WHIT:

Yep. Remember? The kids wanted to start their own radio station, so we set it all up. The station didn't last long, though.

TOM:

Hmmm—that's right. Kid's Radio, you called it.

WHIT:

I got the broadcasting license and everything. (GESTURING TO EQUIPMENT SADLY) Here it sits.

TOM:

Seems like a waste to me.

WHIT:

Me too. But the kids haven't done anything with it.

TOM:

(GETS AN IDEA) Why don't we do our own program—like the old days, the classic stuff?

WHIT:

You mean, like "The Shadow" and "The Lone Ranger"—

TOM:

Jack Benny, Ma Perkins, Fred Allen. The game shows too. Why not?

WHIT:

Hmm.

TOM:

We could recapture that feeling we used to get when our favorite programs would come on the radio. Remember? Kids don't have anything like it now.

WHIT:

True. But . . . I'm not sure kids'll take to radio like that.

TOM:

Sure they will—if it's done right! You have some old scripts lying around, and I don't mind admitting that I have one or two I could wipe the dust off of. A little rehearsal with some of the kids, a few sound effects, and—bingo!—we're back in the old days. Game shows, comedies, dramas, mysteries . . . Whaddaya say?

WHIT:

Well . . . why not? I could hook up the equipment—maybe we should do a special broadcast to let the town know we're back on the air.

TOM:

It could be Odyssey's "Big Broadcast"!

[MUSIC BRIDGES US TO THE NEXT SCENE. IF POSSIBLE, IT SHOULD BEGIN LIKE A NORMAL BRIDGE, BUT TRANSITION INTO A "RADIO ORCHESTRA"—BIG AND EXCESSIVE—FROM THE GOLDEN AGE OF RADIO.]

SCENE 2

[NOW WE'RE LISTENING TO KID'S RADIO. PRODUCTION NOTE: THIS ENTIRE SECTION SHOULD BE VERY REMINISCENT OF THE PRODUCTION QUALITY OF RADIO IN THE '30S AND '40S. IT BEGINS WITH THE "NBC TONES" AND WHIT COMING ON AS ANNOUNCER.]

WHIT:

It's 12 noon and you're listening to "Kid's Radio in Odyssey"—where nothing happens the way you expect!

[WE HEAR A FEW "ORCHESTRATED" STINGS.]

WHIT:

Coming to you live from Whit's End!

[A FEW OCTAVES UP FOR DRAMA]

WHIT:

This hour brought to you by Rinsodent toothpaste! Remember Rinsodent to keep your breath feeling bright and your teeth smelling fresh—

(BEAT) er, your teeth feeling fresh and your—
(BEAT) Remember Rinsodent toothpaste! That's
R-I-N-S-O-Dent in the red and white tube!

[SOME NONDESCRIPT MUSIC]

WHIT:

And now it's time for . . . (WITH HEAVY ECHO)
"Fact or Fiction"—the unconventional contest
that asks that brain-teasing question: "Is it *fact,* or
is it *fiction?*" (KILL ECHO) Featuring your favorite Kid's Radio host—Tom Riley!

[CANNED APPLAUSE THAT CUTS OFF TOO SUDDENLY—CONSISTENTLY. TOM
SHOULD PLAY THIS WITH A PATRONIZING BRAVADO TYPICAL OF THE GAME-
SHOW HOSTS OF THE '30S.]

TOM:

Thank you . . . thank you . . . I'm Tom Riley and
welcome to another exciting edition of "Fact or
Fiction"—the unconventional contest that asks
that brain-teasing question: "Is it *fact,* or is it *fiction?*"

WHIT:

I got that part, Tom.

TOM:

Sorry . . . (TOSSING PAGE ASIDE) wrong script.
(CLEARS THROAT) I'm Tom Riley and welcome
to—oh, forget all that. Whit—who are our
thrilling contestants today?

WHIT:

From right here in Odyssey, our first contestant is
a regular customer at Whit's End and enjoys putting dead lizards in girl's lunchboxes. Ladies and
gentlemen, please welcome our own Jimmy Barclay!

[MUSIC/APPLAUSE]

TOM:

Jimmy, it's good to have you on our show.

JIMMY:

It's good to be here, Mr. Riley.

TOM:

You don't really put dead lizards in girls' lunch-boxes, do you?

JIMMY:

I used to, but I don't anymore.

TOM:

Good for you, Jimmy.

JIMMY:

Dead fish do a better job.

[LAUGHTER]

TOM:

Oh, that crazy Jimmy. And tell us, Whit—who is Jimmy's challenger on today's "Fact or Fiction"?

WHIT:

Well, Tom, it's someone folks in Odyssey know and love. She's a reporter for the "Odyssey Owl" and a regular user of Rinsodent—that's R-I-N-S-O-Dent—as our radio audience will be able to see from her shining smile. We're talking about none other than Lucy Schultz!

[MUSIC/APPLAUSE]

JIMMY:

Her last name is *Schultz?*

TOM:

Hi, Lucy. It's a pleasure to see you.

LUCY:

Thank you, Mr. Riley.

TOM:

Say, you *do* have an awfully nice smile. Do you want to tell our radio audience what you use to keep your teeth so bright and shiny?

JIMMY:

Nail polish remover.

LUCY:

(ASIDE) Quiet, Jimmy. (BEAT) I use Rinsodent, Mr. Riley. Didn't Mr. Whittaker just say so?

19

TOM:

(FLUSTERED, RECOVERING) That's R-I-N-S-O-Dent! Available at fine grocery stores everywhere in Odyssey. And now, on with "Fact or Fiction"—right after this word from our sponsor. Whit?

[BRIEF ORCHESTRA STING]

WHIT:

Well, Tom, we know what the word is—don't we? Yes, that's right. It's Rinsodent toothpaste! Just ask the man in the street which toothpaste he prefers!

[WE HEAR THE SOUND EFFECTS OF A TYPICAL STREET AND TRAFFIC NOISE FADE UP.]

EUGENE:

(ON-MIKE AND SOUNDS AS IF HE'S READING) Yes, Mr. Whittaker, I'm the man in the street, and when somebody asks *me* which toothpaste I used, I say Nine-times-out-of-ten!

WHIT:

(OFF-MIKE) What?

EUGENE:

(TURNS COPY PAGE) Er, nine-times-out-of-ten I'll say "I use Rinsodent! That's R-I-N-S-O-Dent!" It makes my teeth feel white and look fresh! And I—Oh . . .

[MEANWHILE, THE SOUND-EFFECTS RECORDING HAS MOVED ONTO THE NEXT TRACK, AND WE HEAR BARNYARD ANIMALS. THE RECORDING IS SUDDENLY STOPPED.]

WHIT:

Thank you, Mr. Man-in-the-Street. And now, back to "Fact or Fiction"!

TOM:

And now, if our contestants are ready, we'll get on with the first round of "Fact or Fiction." The game is simple. I'll ask a question or make a statement, and you have to tell me whether it's *fact*—or—*fiction*. Lucy, I believe you get the opening question.

LUCY:

Fact!

TOM:

You're absolutely correct! Ten points for Lucy!

[VICTORY MUSIC STING OR BELLS WITH APPLAUSE THAT STOPS ABRUPTLY]

JIMMY:

Hey, wait a minute. That wasn't a question!

LUCY:

Fact again.

TOM:

And Lucy scores another 10 points!

[VICTORY MUSIC STING OR BELLS WITH APPLAUSE THAT STOPS ABRUPTLY]

JIMMY:

Hold on a second!

TOM:

That gives Lucy 15 points to Jimmy's 0.

LUCY:

Fiction!

TOM:

You're right again, Lucy!—because you actually had *20* points to Jimmy's 0! Adding the 10 you've just won, you now have *30* points to Jimmy's 0.

[MORE APPLAUSE CUT OFF SUDDENLY]

TOM:

Come on, Jimmy. You're not trying.

JIMMY:

(DRYLY) Will somebody tell me when the game is supposed to start? I thought we were playing "Fact or Fiction."

TOM:

Fact!

[BELLS, LAUGHTER, APPLAUSE, CUT]

TOM:

Hey, I just won 10 points myself!

JIMMY:

I don't like this game.

LUCY:

Fact!

JIMMY:

Be quiet!

TOM:

And at 40 points Lucy is the big winner of the day! Thanks for joining us. (BEAT) Any last words for our friends at home, Jimmy?

JIMMY:

I was gypped. The game is rigged.

TOM:

(FORCED LAUGH) Oh, that Jimmy—he's such a card. And he needs to be dealt with! (LAUGHS) That's it for now! Thank you for joining us here on "Fact or Fiction"!

[THE CLOSING THEME, EFFECTS, AND AMBIANCE OF THE GAME SHOW GET CUT OFF BY THE SOUND OF AN AP TELETYPE AND THIS SPECIAL REPORT . . .]

WHIT:

(IN THE LOWELL THOMAS TRADITION) We interrupt our regularly scheduled program for a special report . . . This just in from Odyssey City Hall. Mayor Frank Thimplemyer announced today that—

EUGENE:

Uh, excuse me, but we interrupt this special report with our regularly scheduled program. Hasn't anyone ever told you it's *rude* to interrupt?

[GENERIC, UPBEAT SPORTS THEME BEGINS. EUGENE PLAYS THIS CHARACTER AS HIMSELF.]

EUGENE:

And now the "Odyssey Sports Round-Up." I am Eugene Meltsner, and today my special guest is Coach Fred Zachary. Hello, Coach. Thank you for being on the show.

FRED ZACHARY:

It's both a whatchacall honor, privilege, and pleasure to be here, Eugene.

EUGENE:

Shall we talk about this season's team?

FRED ZACHARY:

They're a great group of guys—every one of them.

EUGENE:

Do you have any predictions about what kind of season you'll have?

FRED ZACHARY:

To tell you the truth, it's been my whatchacall experience that you can't tell what a season'll be like until it's over.

EUGENE:

Do you have a particular strategy for the games?

FRED ZACHARY:

Well, my philosophy is that it's not whether you win or lose, but how many points you have at the end.

EUGENE:

How would you compare this season to previous seasons?

FRED ZACHARY:

Frankly, Eugene, the percentages are that 4 times outta 5 our boys are better than half the team they were last season. But I think it's hard to compare two whatchacall separate teams side-by-side. Their similarities are too different to compare.

EUGENE:

What about the fans?

FRED ZACHARY:

Now that's an entirely different subject.

EUGENE:

Oh?

FRED ZACHARY:

Yeah. I think we have the most loyal fans in the county—when they come to the games. If it weren't for the lack of interest, I think we'd see even bigger crowds.

EUGENE:

Coach, I know you are a busy man. Thank you
for taking the time to come down.

FRED ZACHARY:

Hey, I may not have anything to say, but I'll be
glad to talk to you whenever you wanna do an
interview—whether I have time to be here or not.

EUGENE:

You have been listening to "Odyssey's Sports
Round-Up"! I'm Eugene Meltsner. Stay tuned for
the "Odyssey Theatre of the Air"! (OFF-MIKE)
Are we supposed to do a real commercial now or
make one up?

[GENERIC UPBEAT SPORTS THEME TAKES US OUT AND BRIDGES INTO A COMMER-
CIAL BREAK. SOME INCIDENTAL AND VERY INNOCUOUS COMMERCIAL MUSIC.]

WHIT:

(VERY PRESENT AND QUIET.) While we pre-
pare for the next portion of our program, let's go
backstage where two of our performers are talking casually . . .

JIMMY:

(STIFF) Hi, Lucy. You did a really good job on
"Fact or Fiction."

LUCY:

(EQUALLY STIFF.) Thank you, Jimmy. You did
too.

JIMMY:

But I lost.

LUCY:

Yes, but you were a *good* loser. And that's as important as winning.

JIMMY:

Boy, I never thought of it like that before. (BEAT,
OUT OF CHARACTER) Aw, come on, Mr. Whit-
taker. I don't really have to say the rest of this, do
I?

WHIT:

(OFF-MIKE) Jimmy . . .

JIMMY:

But I'd *never* say this to a girl.

WHIT:

You're in character, Jimmy. It isn't *you* talking.

JIMMY:

You got that right.

WHIT:

Then get on with it.

JIMMY:

(STIFF AGAIN) Boy, I never thought of it like that before. You know, Lucy, I like you. You're pretty smart . . . for a girl. [Blah.]

WHIT:

Jimmy . . .

JIMMY:

(SIGHS) All right, all right . . . (STIFF) Tell me something, Lucy.

LUCY:

(STIFF) What, Jimmy?

JIMMY:

Since you're so smart about winning, maybe you can tell me how you keep your skin so clear.

LUCY:

What do you mean, Jimmy?

JIMMY:

Well, Lucy, many kids my age begin to develop unsightly blemishes on their cheeks, noses, and foreheads. But your skin is clear and soft. What is your secret?

LUCY:

My secret is no secret at all . . . I use 100 percent pure "Ivorall"!

JIMMY:

You mean, if *I* use "Ivorall," I'll have clear skin too?

LUCY:

Yes!

JIMMY:

Then I'll try it!

[WE HEAR A XYLOPHONE—INDICATING PASSAGE OF TIME.]

EUGENE:

(PRESENT AND SOFT) Some time later!

LUCY:

(STIFF) Hey, Jimmy, are you ready for the next scene?

JIMMY:

(STIFF) I sure am, Lucy! And even if I don't *win*, I'll look like a winner!

LUCY:

That's swell, Jimmy. How come you're so confident?

JIMMY:

Can't you tell?

LUCY:

It must be due to how clear your skin has become over the past few weeks. What's your secret?

JIMMY:

My secret is no secret at all! I use 100 percent pure "Ivorall"!

[THEY GIGGLE.]

TOM:

(OFF-MIKE, SHUFFLING HIS PAPERS) You gotta keep giggling. I'm not ready yet.

[THEY GIGGLE SOME MORE.]

TOM:

(OFF-MIKE, SHUFFLING HIS PAPERS) Keep going.

[THEY TRY TO FORCE OUT A FEW MORE GIGGLES.]

TOM:

(OFF-MIKE, HE'S READY.) And there we go.

JIMMY:
(OFF-MIKE) I'm never gonna do that again.

[ANOTHER INTERRUPTION OF DRAMATIC NEWS-TYPE MUSIC AND AP TELETYP-
ING.]

WHIT:
(IN THE LOWELL THOMAS TRADITION) We
interrupt this interruption for a special bulletin.

TOM AND EUGENE:
(TO WHIT, ANNOYED) What now?

WHIT:
(FLUSTERED) Oh—ah—nothing. Never mind.

SCENE 3
[BACK TO ODYSSEY'S KID'S RADIO. A "DRAGNET"-TYPE THEME, POSSIBLY DONE
ON AN ORGAN, VERY DETECTIVE-LIKE, AS WHIT INTRODUCES THE PROGRAM.]

WHIT:
The "Odyssey Theatre of the Air" presents . . .

[MUSIC CONTINUES.]

WHIT:
Sam Maritan, Private Eye!

[THE MUSIC SWELLS. WE SEE SAM'S "OFFICE"—A BASIC FIRST-CENTURY DESK AND
CHAIR.]

WHIT:
The time: the first century. The city: Jerusalem.
Who knows what evil lurks in the heart of the
city? Sam doesn't, but he'll take a good guess if
the price is right. Tonight's episode: (HEAVY ON
THE REVERB) "Mystery on the Road to Jericho."

[THE MUSIC PLAYS OUT. WHEN SAM MARITAN IS NARRATING, HE TALKS DIRECT-
LY TO THE AUDIENCE.]

SAM MARITAN:
The name's Maritan. Sam Maritan. My friends
call me Sam. You can call me if you need help.
That's my job: helping people who need help. I'm
a private eye. Yeah, I know what you're thinking:
Nobody likes a private eye. They're cops without

27

badges, men without nerves, heroes without a bank account. Well, that's all right, 'cause I don't need no stinking badges, I can live without nerves, but the bank account—well, that's a different story. In fact, that's *tonight's* story. I call it (HEAVY ON THE REVERB) "Mystery on the Road to Jericho."

[MUSIC STAB]

> SAM MARITAN:
>
> (REGULAR EFFECT) It started when a little Cutie walked into my downtown Jerusalem office.

> LUCY:
>
> Are you Sam Maritan, private eye?

> SAM MARITAN:
>
> Who wants to know?

> LUCY:
>
> My name's Lucy. Lucy Cutie. I'm the youngest in the well-known Cutie family of Jerusalem. Maybe you've heard of us?

> SAM MARITAN:
>
> Who hasn't? What's a little Cutie like you want with a guy like me?

> LUCY:
>
> Help.

> SAM MARITAN:
>
> Then you've come to the right place. What kind of help?

> LUCY:
>
> How many different kinds are there?

> SAM MARITAN:
>
> Plenty, Sister.

> LUCY:
>
> It's not my sister I'm worried about. It's my father. He's missing.

[MUSIC STAB]

SAM MARITAN:

Missing what?

LUCY:

He's not missing anything. *He's* missing.

SAM MARITAN:

I getcha. He's gone . . . vanished . . . kaput . . . splitsville . . .

LUCY:

Yes, he—

SAM MARITAN:

(WITHOUT MISSING A BEAT) . . . hit the road . . . took off . . . disappeared . . .

LUCY:

Yes, he—

SAM MARITAN:

(WITHOUT MISSING A BEAT) . . . took it on the lamb . . . made tracks . . . burned rubber . . .

LUCY:

Yes! Yes! Enough with the overworn cliches!

SAM MARITAN:

I dress the best I can. So—why come to me? Sounds like the police might be more helpful.

LUCY:

I tried the police. All they did was take a report and put his picture on parchments and wine-skins. My family and I are worried. We want someone to find him *now*.

SAM MARITAN:

Wait a minute. Not so fast. How do you know your father doesn't *wanna* be missing?

LUCY:

What do you mean?

SAM MARITAN:

Maybe he decided he was tired of you little Cuties. Maybe he found a *new* Cutie?

[MUSIC STAB]

29

LUCY:

You think he's staying with relatives?

SAM MARITAN:

Never mind.

LUCY:

We want you to find him—*wherever* he is. And we're willing to pay handsomely for it.

SAM MARITAN:

Detective Handsomely went out of business years ago. You gotta pay *me* if you want me to look for your dad. But it won't be cheap.

LUCY:

We Cuties never do anything *cheap*. I've got two silver coins. You want them? (SHE DROPS THE TWO COINS ON THE TABLE.)

SAM MARITAN:

Ha. You think you can buy me with two little silver coins?

LUCY:

Yes.

SAM MARITAN:

You're right. (HE PICKS UP THE COINS.) Give me the facts. When did your father leave, and where was he headed?

LUCY:

He left last night and was going from Jerusalem to Jericho. That's all we know.

SAM MARITAN:

All right. I'll get on it. But tell me something, Cutie—the name Sam Maritan turns a lot of people off in this town. You could've gone to any of the native detectives. Why'd you pick me? Was it my reputation for fast and efficient work?

LUCY:

No. You're the only one who has hours on Saturday.

[BRIDGE MUSIC. SAM GETS UP FROM DESK AND MOVES TO ONE SIDE. HE HAS HOLD OF SOME REINS THAT STRETCH OUT OF SIGHT—THE IDEA BEING THAT THERE'S A MULE OFFSTAGE THAT WE CAN'T SEE.]

SAM MARITAN:

(NARRATOR) With that vote of confidence, I got started on the case. In no time at all I learned two things. First: the father left last night. Second: he was going down the road from Jerusalem to Jericho. I decided the best course of action would be to retrace his journey. I climbed onto my late model turbo-injected mule and took off . . .

[WE HEAR THE MULE BRAYING.]

SAM MARITAN:

. . . *after* I pulled him for two miles.

[LIGHT MUSIC. SAM WALKS AROUND THE STAGE, LOOKING FOR CLUES AS HE TALKS.]

SAM MARITAN:

(NARRATOR) In case you're not familiar with the road to Jericho, it has a history of danger and mystery. (Hey, that rhymes.) I guess that's why this is called the (HEAVY ON THE REVERB) "Mystery on the Road to Jericho."

[MUSIC STAB]

SAM MARITAN:

(NORMAL AGAIN) Boy, I love that sound. (BEAT) The road itself is OK—good quality dirt, not a lot of potholes—but it's lined with a lot of bushes and hills. Good hiding places. Especially if you're a bandit or hedge robber. Why anyone would want to rob the hedges, I don't know, but it's a funny world we live in. After what seemed like hours, I pulled into a roadside cafe.

[WE HEAR BRAYING MIXED WITH THE SOUND OF A CAR SCREECHING TO A HALT. THE LOBBY CAN BE A BASIC DESK FOR THE RECEPTIONIST, A FEW CHAIRS, ETC., AND A "JUKEBOX" IN THE CORNER (NOT ABSOLUTELY NECESSARY).]

SAM MARITAN:

I was on my way into the lobby when I saw one of the town's religious leaders riding along on a donkey. I had an idea. (BEAT, CALLS OFF-STAGE) Excuse me, O Liturgical One.

FIRST PRIEST:
(AS PRIEST-TYPE, ENTERS) Yes? May I help
you?

SAM MARITAN:
That depends. You've just come from Jericho,
haven't you?

FIRST PRIEST:
I did. How could you tell?

SAM MARITAN:
My keen sense of deduction, my brilliant percep-
tiveness, and . . .

FIRST PRIEST:
The "I Love Jericho" bumper sticker on the back
of my donkey.

SAM MARITAN:
Exactly. What was your business there?

FIRST PRIEST:
I was attending the Annual Religious Leaders'
Convention at the Jericho Inn.

SAM MARITAN:
You guys have a convention?

FIRST PRIEST:
Oh yes . . . we sit around the pool and sing con-
troversial theological songs. It's a lot of fun.

SAM MARITAN:
(SARCASTICALLY) Sure sounds like it. Tell me—
on your way back, you didn't happen to see a
man, did you?

FIRST PRIEST:
(SUSPICIOUSLY) A man?

SAM MARITAN:
Yes, a man. You know the type: head, body, arms
and legs.

FIRST PRIEST:
I might've seen one or two.

SAM MARITAN:

(SHOWS HIM A PARCHMENT) Take a look at this parchment. Did you see a man who resembled the face in this drawing?

FIRST PRIEST:

(TOO QUICKLY) No! I didn't!

SAM MARITAN:

But you haven't even looked at the drawing.

FIRST PRIEST:

I don't have to! I haven't seen him! Now leave me alone! I'm tired and I'm late getting back to Jerusalem!

SAM MARITAN:

Yeah, I guess all that poolside singing must wear you out. (GETTING TOUGH) Come on, I think you know something.

FIRST PRIEST:

I'm a religious leader, young man—you can't expect me to know anything!

SAM MARITAN:

No comment. (BEAT) You've seen this man, haven't you!

FIRST PRIEST:

No! And even if I did, he was beaten and half-dead and I couldn't have helped him anyway. Now go away and leave me alone! (GOES OFF-STAGE, DROPPING A SMALL JAR AS HE GOES. WE HEAR HIM KICKING THE DONKEY.) Yah! Get on Balaam!

[THE DONKEY GRUNTS, AND THE PRIEST RIDES OFF. THE LEVITE ENTERS AND GOES OVER TO A "JUKEBOX" IN THE CORNER.]

SAM MARITAN:

Hmmm . . . strange behavior. (NARRATOR) One of the marks of a good private detective—besides the five o'clock shadow and bloodshot eyes—is that he picks up on little things. The kinds of things no one else would pick up. Like the small jar of oil the priest dropped on the ground as he left. (PICKS UP JAR, READING.) "Oil of OK—

33

Courtesy of the Jericho Inn." (BEAT) I'll bet he swiped their towels too. (NARRATOR) Since I stopped at the roadside cafe, I thought I'd have a quick drink—of water. (IN THE SCENE, AT THE COUNTER) Where's the innkeeper?

INNKEEPER:

Yeah? What do you want?

SAM MARITAN:

I want the innkeeper.

INNKEEPER:

You're looking at him.

SAM MARITAN:

Aren't you a little young to be an innkeeper?

INNKEEPER:

No. The Youngs run the place across the street. I'm a little Small, though. What can I get you?

SAM MARITAN:

Well, Mr. Small. (PULLING OUT PARCHMENT) You can get me a glass of water and tell me if you've seen the man on this parchment.

INNKEEPER:

I can help you with the water but can't with the man. I haven't seen him. Has he been through here?

SAM MARITAN:

That's the story. He was going from Jerusalem to Jericho.

INNKEEPER:

Sorry, pal. But that gentleman across the room might know something.

SAM MARITAN:

Who—where?

INNKEEPER:

There by the jukebox. The Levite. He just came from Jericho.

SAM MARITAN:

Thanks. (NARRATOR) I walked over to the Levite and tapped him on the shoulder. (IN THE SCENE) Hey, bub.

LEVITE:

(VERY PRISSY AND UPPER CLASS) Don't touch me, peasant.

SAM MARITAN:

I'm not a peasant—I'm Sam Maritan, private eye, and I have some questions for you.

LEVITE:

(DISDAINFULLY) Sam Maritan . . . private eye? You'd be better off a peasant. Go away. I have nothing to say to you.

SAM MARITAN:

Look, pal, there's a missing man and I've been hired to find him. Little Small over there thinks you can help. (SHOWS HIM THE PARCHMENT) Take a look at this parchment. You ever seen this guy before?

LEVITE:

(BORED) If it will make you go away, I'll look. (LOOKS) No, I've never seen the—(GASPS VERY AUDIBLY AS HE SUDDENLY RECOGNIZES HIM)

[MUSIC STAB]

SAM MARITAN:

What? What is it? You've seen him.

LEVITE:

No! This jukebox doesn't have any classical music. Now go away.

SAM MARITAN:

Forget it, Mr. High-and-mighty. You recognized the man in the picture.

LEVITE:

It's getting late. I want to leave.

SAM MARITAN:

Aw, no, you don't. That's what the religious leader did! (GRABS HIM) You're gonna tell me where you've seen this guy!

LEVITE:

You can't bully me!

SAM MARITAN:

Oh yeah? Just watch. Should I start with rude names or go straight to an editorial in the "Jerusalem Times"?

LEVITE:

(THREATENED, BLUBBERING FROM FRIGHT) No! You wouldn't! You have nothing on me! I was only riding past!

SAM MARITAN:

Past what? Spill it, Levite!

LEVITE:

He . . . he was on the side of the road. I didn't think he was alive . . . When he called out, it . . . it frightened me. He was beaten and . . . I didn't want to get involved . . . Who knows where he's been!

SAM MARITAN:

(DISGUSTED) Uh huh. You saw a man in need and —what? You rode by at an incredible high speed?

LEVITE:

No! (BEAT) I couldn't get my donkey to go at an incredibly high speed, so I went by on the other side of the road.

SAM MARITAN:

Shoulda figured. And I'll bet the religious guy did the same thing. What's this world coming to—when people won't bother helping people in trouble? You should be ashamed.

LEVITE:

(REGAINING HIS COMPOSURE) I have nothing else to say to you.

SAM MARITAN:

You've said plenty, pal. Plenty.

[MUSIC BRIDGE. THE LEVITE SLINKS OFF.]

SAM MARITAN:
(NARRATOR) I jumped on Old Turbo—

[PICKS UP THE REINS AND PULLS AT THEM AGAIN. BRAYING OFFSTAGE AS HE SPEAKS.]

SAM MARITAN:
—and took off for Jericho. I kept my eyes peeled for my missing man. Sure enough, I found him further up on the side of the road.

[MUSIC STAB]

SAM MARITAN:
It didn't take a genius to figure out what happened to him. (Which is a good thing for me.) He had been robbed, beaten, stripped of his clothes, and left for dead. I wondered how many people passed by him and refused to help. I couldn't help but wonder if, under different circumstances, *I* would've passed by too. (PAUSE) I remembered the Oil of OK I had stuffed in my pouch and rubbed it on him to help soothe the pain of his cuts. Then I picked him up, put him on Old Turbo, and took him back to the roadside cafe.

[SAM MARITAN GOES OFFSTAGE AND RETURNS WITH THE WOUNDED MAN. GENTLY LAYS HIM DOWN BY THE RECEPTION DESK.]

INNKEEPER:
Hey, wait a minute. I'm a cafe, not a hospital! What do you want me to do with him?

SAM MARITAN:
He needs help, can'tja see?

INNKEEPER:
So who doesn't? I wanna know who's gonna take care of the room service!

SAM MARITAN:
(GROWLS) Look, Skinflint, I've got two silver coins—more than enough to take care of anything he needs. Keep him here while I go back to Jerusalem. I'll pay you anything else you want when I come back. Got it?

INNKEEPER:
Money talks, my man. Money talks.

[LIGHT MUSIC BED BEGINS.]

SAM MARITAN:
(NARRATOR) I went back to Jerusalem and told
the rest of the Cuties that their father was found.
We went back to the roadside cafe together,
where I witnessed a happy family reunion. I
slipped away quietly. Never did get the two sil-
ver coins back. But it didn't matter. I think I got
something more important. A good story called
(HEAVY ON THE REVERB) "Mystery on the—"
(BEAT, NORMAL EFFECT) Nah. Forget it.
There's a guy I know who tells the story better,
and *He* calls it the Parable of the Good Samaritan.
Maybe you've heard it? (BEAT) Till next time, I'm
Sam Maritan, private eye!

[MUSIC PLAYS OUT TO BIG FINISH.]

WHIT:
You've been listening to "Odyssey's Theatre of
the Air" and another exciting episode of . . . Sam
Maritan, Private Eye! (BEAT) That concludes our
program for today. Thank you for listening to . . .
Kid's Radio!

[MUSIC CONCLUDES WITH A BIG FINISH—SERVING AS A BRIDGE TO THE NEXT
SCENE.]

SCENE 4
[AND WE ARE NOW BEHIND THE SCENES OF KID'S RADIO.]

WHIT:
(SIGH OF RELIEF) Well, that was pretty good, if I
may say so myself. Good job, Eugene.

EUGENE:
Thank you, Mr. Whittaker.

WHIT:
You too, Tom . . .

TOM:
Uh huh.

WHIT:

Lucy . . . you little Cutie.

LUCY:

You don't think I'll be locked into a stereotype do you?

WHIT:

There are worse stereotypes, Lucy. Jimmy, you did a—(BEAT) Jimmy?

JIMMY:

(BREATHLESS) Sorry, Mr. Whittaker! You gotta see it! Connie says the phone's been ringing off the hook. Everybody *loves* Kid's Radio!

WHIT:

That's great, Jimmy.

EUGENE:

You mean people have really been listening?

TOM:

See, Whit? What did I tell you? Huh?

WHIT:

You were right, Tom. Only one problem . . .

TOM:

What?

WHIT:

That was all right for a half hour, but . . . how are we going to fill the rest of the 23 and a half hours in the day?

TOM:

Oops . . . I hadn't thought of that.

[PLAYFUL MUSIC BED BEGINS.]

EUGENE:

I could do a lecture on the fundamentals of electrical conductivity . . .

LUCY:

I have some poems I could read.

39

JIMMY:
I could play some kind of superhero . . .

TOM:
Come to think of it, I could show some home
movies from my trip to Cleveland.

ALL:
Cleveland!

[THE MUSIC TAKES US OUT OF THE EPISODE . . . AND TO THE END.]

By Faith, Noah . . .

INTRODUCTION

By Faith, Noah . . . originally aired on January 7, 1989, as the kick-off for a 12-episode series exploring the basics of Christianity. The title comes from Hebrews 11:7, where the writer gives Noah his place in that wonderful "Hall of Fame of Faith."

The humorous style of this program is one we used again and again in *Adventures in Odyssey*, showing up mostly in our Kid's Radio (see the rest of the scripts in this collection) and "B-TV" episodes.

PRODUCTION NOTES

There will be suggestions throughout the script for staging and production ideas.

Scene 1—the fictitious drama—could be done live on the stage (if you have the room and equipment to pull it off) or live offstage during the blackout, or simply prerecord it on tape and play it during the blackout.

Scene 2 can take place off to one side of the stage, isolated by a spotlight, or in front of the curtain with our three characters sitting on the "soda shop" stools. Then, when they move into the next scene, the curtain can open or the lights come up more fully to reveal the Bible Room.

The Bible Room, by the way, is a museum-type room filled with displays to help bring the Bible to life for children. You can use your imagination about how to design the set, but the radio program has referred to such attractions as a "Talking Mirror" (you start a Bible verse and the mirror helps you finish it), a set of armor to illustrate the "full armor of God," a representation of the walls of Jericho, a display of Samson bringing down the temple, the popular Imagination Station (which seems to send kids "back in time" to important events in history) and the Room of Consequence (allowing kids to see what *might* happen if they play out a particular decision).

The rest of the scenes involving Noah can take place in the Bible Room, with very minor adjustments to the set.

CAST OF CHARACTERS

JOHN AVERY WHITTAKER: *our storyteller; a wise and insightful man*

JACK: *a "typical" boy*

LUCY: *a sharp and perceptive girl*

NOAH: *an old and faithful man*

NOAH'S WIFE: *an old and somewhat beleaguered woman*

A Man in the Crowd

Another Man in the Crowd

A Woman in the Crowd

Fro-Jiday, the Health Inspector: *a Jack Webb, no-nonsense type*

Macthuselah, the Union Official: *a rather gruff, blue-collar type*

Jared Rumbottom, Attorney: *a civil-liberties type*

Woman from the Animal Rights Group

Policeman

Japheth: *Noah's son*

SCENE 1
[DRAMATICALLY AND MUSICALLY, WE ARE IN THE MIDDLE OF A GREAT ADVENTURE. WE HEAR A HOUSE BURNING, MIXED VOICES OF PANIC AND CONFUSION. IN THE DISTANCE, SIRENS. WHIT NARRATES FOR US. IF YOU HAVE ROOM ON YOUR STAGE FOR A BOY TO STAND AT A WINDOW (WITH THE RIGHT KIND OF LIGHTING EFFECTS BEHIND TO ILLUSTRATE A FIRE), THE FATHER IN THIS SCENE COULD BE A VOICE DOWNSTAGE. OTHERWISE, YOU MAY WANT TO HAVE WHIT NARRATE ON-STAGE, BUT HAVE BILLY AND HIS FATHER'S VOICE (WITH SOUND EFFECTS) OFF-STAGE. OR YOU COULD PRERECORD THIS LIKE A RADIO DRAMA AND DO IT DURING A BLACKOUT, BEFORE THE CURTAIN RISES.]

WHIT:
The fire blazed through the house, pushing little
Billy to his bedroom window on the second floor.
He looked down and saw his parents, who had
been frantically trying to find him.

BILLY:
Daddy! Daddy! Help!

FATHER:
Billy!

[WE HEAR THE CRASH OF FLOORING SOMEWHERE IN THE HOUSE. THE MUSIC BEGINS BUILDING TO A DRAMATIC CLIMAX.]

BILLY:
I can't get down, Daddy! Help!

FATHER:
Jump, Billy! I'll catch you!

42

BILLY:

It's too high! I . . . I'm afraid!

FATHER:

Don't be afraid, Billy! Jump! Jump into my arms!

BILLY:

But, Dad . . .

[ANOTHER CRASH, THE MUSIC REACHING ITS PEAK]

FATHER:

Jump, Billy! Juuuuuummmp!

[WITH A STUNNING ABRUPTNESS, EVERYTHING IS SILENT FOR A MOMENT. CURTAIN OR SPOT TO REVEAL OUR THREE CHARACTERS.]

JACK:

Well, Mr. Whittaker?

WHIT:

Well what, Jack?

JACK:

That's your story about the meaning of faith?

WHIT:

Yep.

JACK:

I don't get it.

WHIT:

You don't? Hmmm . . . how about you, Lucy?

LUCY:

Ummmm . . . I could guess, so maybe you should just tell us.

WHIT:

(CHUCKLES) You see, the real meaning of faith is *trust*. Like in our story, Little Billy may have always said he trusted his father—had *faith* in him—but now he's faced with a situation where his faith has to be made *real*. As long as Billy stays up in the burning room, he's showing that he *doesn't* have enough faith to jump in his father's arms. A real and active faith can't begin until his feet have left the windowsill.

43

LUCY:

Is that what they mean when they call it a "leap of faith"?

WHIT:

I suppose so.

JACK:

Wow.

WHIT:

Now the real question is: would *you* have jumped?

JACK:

Nah.

LUCY:

You wouldn't?

JACK:

No way. My dad has skinny arms. He'd drop me like a hot potato.

WHIT:

(CHUCKLES) Well, I'm not so sure about that, but that's the other important point about faith: you have to be sure you're putting it in the right person. You want to trust someone who'll do what he says he'll do.

JACK:

You're talking about God, right?

WHIT:

Right.

JACK:

But we can't see *Him*.

WHIT:

That's why sometimes it takes more faith.

LUCY:

The kids at school say I'm crazy for believing in Someone I can't see.

JACK:

Yeah. At least in your story, Billy could see his Dad down there. It's different in real life. I mean, it's hard to really have faith in somebody you can't see.

WHIT:

Funny you should mention that. Come on up to the Bible Room, and I'll tell you about someone who *did* . . .

[MUSIC BRIDGE TO THE NEXT SCENE AS OUR THREE CHARACTERS MOVE INTO THE BIBLE ROOM SET.]

SCENE 2
[THE BIBLE ROOM. IN THE CENTER IS A STRUCTURE THAT COULD/SHOULD APPEAR TO BE A LARGE BOAT. THE ARK, IN FACT.]

LUCY:

I love this room.

JACK:

It's different every time I come in. (BEAT) Oh— look at that big boat! What's that for?

WHIT:

Ah, here we are. (PULLING BIBLE FROM THE SHELF, FLIPPING THROUGH THE PAGES TO:) Hebrews chapter 11 says: "Now faith is the assurance of things hoped for, the conviction of things not seen" . . . then, in verse 7: "By faith, Noah, being warned by God about things not seen, moved with godly fear, prepared an ark for the saving of his household, by which he condemned the world, and became an heir of the righteousness which is according to faith." Sit down, Jack, Lucy . . . let me tell you about this fellow named Noah . . .

JACK:

I've heard about him. He built the ark.

LUCY:

Everybody's heard about Noah, Jack. But it's different when you hear about him in the Bible Room. Tell us the story, Mr. Whittaker.

[THEY MAKE THEMSELVES COMFORTABLE OFF TO ONE SIDE OF THE STAGE.]

WHIT:

Well, Noah lived hundreds of years ago at a time when people had become especially wicked. The Bible says that every intent of the thoughts of their hearts was on evil continually. "And the Lord was sorry that He had made man on the earth and He was grieved in His heart."

JACK:

Things must've been pretty terrible to make God feel that bad.

WHIT:

They sure were. So God decided to destroy man and the animals and even the creeping things—

LUCY:

I wish He'd get rid of the creeping things *now*.

JACK:

Quiet, Lucy. (TO WHIT) He decided to get rid of *everybody*, Mr. Whittaker?

WHIT:

Obviously not everybody or we wouldn't be here now. But there was one man in particular . . .

LUCY:

Noah.

WHIT:

That's right. According to the Bible, "Noah found grace in the sight of the Lord . . . He was a just man, perfect in his time. Noah walked with God."

LUCY:

He actually *walked* with God? Like Jack and I walk together to school?

WHIT:

Some think so. Others believe it's a figure of speech: he walked with God in the sense that he obeyed God and had a close relationship with Him. So God chose Noah to be a part of a very special plan. Though the Bible doesn't say exactly what happened over those years, we can imagine how it must have affected his life . . .

[WE ARE IN NOAH'S HOUSE—A WOODEN TABLE AND A COUPLE OF CHAIRS SHOULD SUFFICE—AT THE END OF WHAT WOULD SEEM TO BE A NORMAL DAY. NOAH COMES THROUGH THE FRONT DOOR. HIS WIFE COMES FROM THE KITCHEN TO GREET HIM.]

NOAH:

Honey, I'm home!

WIFE:

Hello, Dear. (SHE KISSES HIM.) How was your day?

NOAH:

Not bad. I worked on our vineyards in the north-west corner, planted a new field of crops, and talked to God. What's for dinner?

WIFE:

Oh, is that all? Well— (BEAT) You talked to God? You talked to *God*, and you're asking me, "What's for dinner?" Sit down. We talk first, then dinner.

[THEY SIT DOWN.]

WIFE:

Why did God want to talk to you? Is everything all right?

NOAH:

Not really. God said He was grieved in His heart about all the wickedness going on around here.

WIFE:

He should live in *our* neighborhood, He wants to see wickedness.

NOAH:

He told me about His plan to destroy all of mankind and all of the animals. Where's today's paper? I wanna see who won the game. (NOAH PICKS UP A NEWSPAPER, RIFFLES THROUGH IT.)

WIFE:

Stop with the paper. God's gonna destroy man and the animals?

NOAH:

That's what He said.

47

WIFE:

I wonder if I should cancel my hair appointment next Saturday. When is this supposed to happen?

NOAH:

He didn't say exactly.

WIFE:

Then why did the Lord tell you these things? If He's going to destroy all of mankind and the animals, that would include us, right? I mean, we're not a family of radishes.

NOAH:

There's the catch. The Lord gave me some instructions about how we can be saved from the destruction. He wants me to build a very big boat: an *ark*.

WIFE:

An ark, huh? I guess this means He won't be destroying the earth with a sandstorm.

NOAH:

Nope. The Lord said—and I quote: "Behold, I myself am bringing the flood of waters on the earth, to destroy from under heaven all flesh in which is the breath of life, and everything that is on the earth shall die. But I will establish my covenant with you, and you shall go into the ark—you, your sons, your wife, and your son's wives with you."

WIFE:

God is very merciful to save us—but why a big boat? We're a small family, couldn't we just float around on a raft?

NOAH:

Well, that's the other catch. God told me to bring two of every living thing on the ark with us, male and female.

WIFE:

He wants you to bring animals and birds on this boat?

NOAH:

That's what He said—I'm not going to argue.
And we also have to gather enough food for
them and us to eat. Speaking of food—

WIFE:

So we have to feed them too. As if I don't have
enough housework to do.

NOAH:

Imagine it, Darling. I get to be a shipbuilder,
sailor, and a zookeeper.

WIFE:

Eh. You're only 480 years old, what's a new career?

NOAH:

So tell me—do you have dinner ready, or do I sit
here starving to death before I get to 481?

[BACK TO THE BIBLE ROOM]

WHIT:

And Noah did all that the Lord commanded him.

JACK:

Wow. That's *a lot* of work. Building an ark, collecting the animals . . . I hope God gave him some
time. It took me all summer to build a tree fort.

LUCY:

I had to do a butterfly collection in *three weeks* last
year.

JACK:

How long did it take Noah to build the ark, Mr.
Whittaker?

WHIT:

Some people figure it took about 120 years.

JACK:

Oh, that's not bad. (BEAT) *A hundred and twenty
years!*

WHIT:

Yep. And don't forget—that's 120 years doing
work for Someone Noah *hasn't* seen, to save him
from something that *hasn't* happened.

LUCY:

That's faith.

WHIT:

Exactly. You said you got picked on at school. It's very likely Noah got picked on too. See, in 2 Peter 2:5, we're told that Noah *preached* to his people. Imagine it!

[SOME OF TOWNSPEOPLE HAVE GATHERED AROUND NOAH WHILE HE'S WORKING ON THE BOAT.]

NOAH:

Listen, folks, I'm telling you, there's going to be water everywhere. God's judgment is coming. You've got to turn away from your wickedness.

MAN:

Yaddah—yaddah—yaddah. You've been saying this for 100 years, Noah.

NOAH:

A hundred? I'll say it for a thousand! God said it's going to happen, and happen it will. I'm talking lots of water here.

ANOTHER MAN:

The only water I see is the sweat on your brow from building that stupid boat. Get a grip, will you? You've become the town laughingstock.

NOAH:

Laugh then—all of you. But God isn't, and neither am I.

WOMAN IN CROWD:

I wouldn't laugh either if I had all those animals running around *my* backyard!

[THEY FIND THIS AMUSING.]

NOAH:

I'd rather be an animal waiting for safety than a fool who waits for destruction.

MAN:

Oh, well, aren't *you* the one with the wise words all of a sudden! Come on, gang, let's get away from this whacko.

[THE CROWD EXITS TO MAKE ROOM FOR THE NEXT CROWD.]

WHIT:

And though the Bible doesn't give us the details, we can guess that Noah had *other* problems too.

[WE HEAR A NEW CROWD ARGUING, SHOUTING AT NOAH.]

NOAH:

Hold it! Hold it! Quiet please!

[THEY QUIET DOWN.]

NOAH:

Thank you. Now, who are you people and what are you doing at my back gate? (TO THE IN-SPECTOR) You there. What do you want?

[WE MEET THE TOWN HEALTH INSPECTOR, WHO SOUNDS A LOT LIKE JACK WEBB FROM "DRAGNET." IN THE BACKGROUND WE HEAR A VARIETY OF ANIMAL NOIS-ES AND ARK CONSTRUCTION.]

INSPECTOR:

Are you Noah, son of Lamech, father of Shem, Ham, and Japheth?

NOAH:

That's me.

INSPECTOR:

The name's Fro-Jiday. City Health Inspector Fro-Jiday. We seem to have a problem here.

NOAH:

You're telling me! Look at what you've done to my rose garden! I've had elephants for 15 years, and they show more respect. My wife is not going to be a happy woman.

INSPECTOR:

I see. You've got bigger problems than that, I'm afraid. I have a list of citations against you.

NOAH:

Citations? What citations?

INSPECTOR:

Unauthorized construction, housing animals—well, let's take this one at a time . . .

NOAH:

I'm taking them two at a time, actually.

INSPECTOR:

Whatever. First, you've been constructing this . . . this . . . what do you call this thing?

NOAH:

An ark.

INSPECTOR:

An ark. Correct. Do you have a building permit for this thing?

NOAH:

No. Technically, it's not a building. It's a boat.

INSPECTOR:

I see. Do you have a boat permit, then?

NOAH:

I need a boat permit?

INSPECTOR:

You've been building this for over a hundred years and didn't know you needed a permit? Ignorance of the law is no excuse. (RIPPING PAPER FROM A PAD) Here. Maybe this citation will remind you to get one. Tell me, is this little yacht for business or pleasure?

NOAH:

Ah . . . I don't know.

INSPECTOR:

What are you gonna do with this thing? You gonna go scuba diving? Water skiing? Fishing?

NOAH:

It's for safety.

INSPECTOR:

Safety?

NOAH:

Yeah. The world's going to be destroyed by water, and this ark will protect me and my family.

INSPECTOR:

Destroyed by water? Are you going to be responsible for this?

NOAH:

No. God's going to do it.

INSPECTOR:

Hmmm . . . I'll have to talk to Him about that. You need a water usage permit before you can do something like that.

UNION MAN:

Step aside—forget this permit nonsense. I've got something more important here.

NOAH:

Who are you?

UNION MAN:

Macthuselah. I'm head of the Ark Builders Union Number 407. You and your boys are not members. We don't look kindly on non-union people doing our work. What do you think unions are for?

NOAH:

Look, what do I know from union and non-union? We're a family operation here.

UNION MAN:

Yeah, that figures. Giving rank and privilege to your children! What about equal opportunity? What about all the other qualified boat builders?

NOAH:

I've been *giving* everyone equal opportunity! Turn from your wicked ways, and you can come help.

ATTORNEY:

Just what I've been suspecting. You're trying to impose your morality on those around you.

NOAH:

And who are you?

ATTORNEY:

I'm Jared Rumbottom from the Pre-antediluvian
Civil Liberties Association. What you're doing is
against the city's constitution. I'm going to repre-
sent anyone and everyone you've offended, sue
you, and make you go broke in court costs.

NOAH:

This is getting awfully ridiculous.

WOMAN ANIMAL RIGHTS:

Wait just a minute! I'm from the Society for the
Protection of Cruel Animals, and I want to see
your authorization for keeping these pooorrrr
hapless creatures caged up in your backyard.

NOAH:

Caged up? They have more room now than when
I found them! (FIRMLY) Listen, folks, I want you
to get out of my yard before I call the police!

POLICEMAN:

I *am* the police. Do you realize your ark over
there is double-parked?

NOAH:

Oh, brother . . .

[THE ARGUMENT CONTINUES BETWEEN ALL OF THESE CHARACTERS AS WE GO
BACK TO THE BIBLE ROOM.]

LUCY:

(SUSPICIOUSLY) Wait a minute, Mr. Whittaker
. . . it didn't *really* happen that way, did it?

WHIT:

(CHUCKLING) The Bible doesn't say *exactly*, but,
like I told you, we're just using our imaginations.

JACK:

Don't worry about it, Lucy. Go on with the story,
Mr. Whittaker.

WHIT:

Noah worked hard building the ark, collecting
the animals, and trying in vain to get the people
to give up their wickedness. Then the Lord said
to Noah, "Come into the ark, you and all your

household, because I have seen that you are righteous before Me in this generation." So Noah, his family, and all the various numbers of animals went aboard the finished ark. And God closed the door behind them.

[THE DOOR OF THE ARK SLAMS SHUT, FOLLOWED BY A THUNDEROUS CRASH AND THE BEGINNING OF THE RAINFALL.]

WHIT:

After seven days, the waters of the flood were on the earth. All the fountains of the deep were broken up, and the windows of heaven were opened. And the rain was on the earth 40 days and 40 nights. The waters increased and lifted the ark high above the earth, even above the highest hills. (SOBERLY, MORE OMINOUSLY) And, just as He promised, God destroyed all living things on the ground. Only Noah and those who were with him in the ark remained alive.

SCENE 3
[BACK TO THE BIBLE ROOM]

WHIT:

So you see—there's an example of a man who had faith in God—enough faith to do what God had told him to do, even though he couldn't see God. "By faith Noah, being divinely warned of things not seen, moved with godly fear, prepared an ark for the saving of his household, by which he condemned the world and became heir of the righteousness which is according to faith."

JACK:

Wow.

LUCY:

But that's not the end, Mr. Whittaker. You have to finish it!

WHIT:

Don't you know the end?

LUCY:

Yeah—but I want to hear it anyway.

55

WHIT:

Oh—all right. Where were we?

JACK:

They were all on the ark, floating on the water—
the only people in the whole world left alive.

WHIT:

That's right . . .

[WE ARE INSIDE OF THE ARK—THE FAMILY AREA—AND HEAR THE SOFT LAPPING OF WAVES AGAINST THE ARK'S SIDES. MUFFLED, IN THE INTERNALS OF THE ARK, WE HEAR THE SOUNDS OF VARIOUS ANIMALS.]

NOAH:

Japheth! Bring me a raven!

JAPHETH:

Yes, Father!

NOAH:

(TO HIMSELF) We've been on this ark for nearly
half a year—good thing I don't get seasick.

[JAPHETH BRINGS A BOX. WE HEAR THE SQUAWKING OF A RAVEN INSIDE.]

JAPHETH:

Here's the raven, Father.

NOAH:

Thank you, Son. Open that window, will you
please?

JAPHETH:

Yes, sir.

[WE HEAR THE SOUND OF A WINDOW BEING OPENED—PROBABLY SHUTTERS, AC-TUALLY. THIS MIGHT BE ACCOMPLISH BY HAVING NOAH MOVE TOWARD THE EDGE OF STAGE LEFT OR RIGHT SO THAT HIS ARMS, WHEN HE OPENS THE BOX, WILL BE OUT OF SIGHT.]

NOAH:

O Lord, thank You for not forgetting us, your ser-
vants. Just as you have caused the wind to pass
over the earth, so the waters are finally draining
away. We appreciate it. Amen. (BEAT) All right,
my little raven. Fly! (HE LETS THE RAVEN GO;
IT FLIES OFF.) Fly to dry ground if you can find it!

[BACK TO WHIT AS NARRATOR]

WHIT:

The raven flew, going to and fro, but returning to
the ark because he couldn't find a place to land.

[WE HEAR THE COOING OF A DOVE INSIDE ANOTHER BOX.]

JAPHETH:

Here's the dove you asked for, Father.

NOAH:

Thank you, Son. Open that window, will you
please?

JAPHETH:

Yes, sir.

[WE HEAR THE SOUND OF A WINDOW BEING OPENED, AS BEFORE.]

NOAH:

Well, Lord, the raven couldn't find anything. But
You're still draining the water from all the earth,
and I believe the time is coming when we'll see
land again. Thank You for taking care of us.
Amen. (BEAT) All right, my little dove. Fly! (HE
LETS THE DOVE GO; IT FLIES OFF.) Fly to dry
ground if you can find it! (I hope you do better
than the raven.)

[BACK TO WHIT AS NARRATOR]

WHIT:

But the dove found no resting place for the sole of
her foot, and she returned to the ark to Noah. So
Noah waited for seven days and tried again . . .

NOAH:

Japheth!

JAPHETH:

(ENTERS WITH BOX) I know, I know—a dove.
Are you sure you don't want to try the raven
again?

NOAH:

Nah—we'll stick with the dove. Thank you, and
would you—?

JAPHETH:

The window. I've got it.

NOAH:

Lord, if there's any dry ground out there, please let this dove find it. Amen. (BEAT) All right, my little dove—well, you know the routine. (HE LETS THE DOVE GO; IT FLIES OFF.) Maybe I should try the parakeet.

[BACK TO WHIT AS NARRATOR]

WHIT:

But this time the dove came back in the evening with a freshly plucked olive leaf in her mouth— and Noah knew the waters were almost gone.

NOAH:

You don't have to be a genius to figure some of this stuff out.

WHIT:

In seven days, he sent the dove out again. The dove did not return. And it came to pass that the surface of the ground became dry. Then God spoke to Noah, saying, "Go out of the ark, you and your family and all of the animals, and be fruitful and multiply on the earth." And they did.

LUCY:

Don't forget the rainbow.

WHIT:

I wouldn't forget that.

JACK:

What rainbow?

WHIT:

Noah built an altar to the Lord and presented burnt offerings. The Lord was so pleased He promised that He would never destroy the earth by water again. And God placed a rainbow in the sky and said, "I set My rainbow in the cloud, and it shall be a sign of the promise between Me and the earth. And when I see the rainbow, I'll remember what I've promised." And it's a way for us to remember God's promise too.

[FOR THIS PREVIOUS SPEECH, YOU MAY WANT TO ASSEMBLE NOAH AND HIS FAMILY ON STAGE, LOOKING OUT IN AWE OVER THE AUDIENCE AS IF THEY SEE A RAINBOW.]

JACK:

Wow. What a story!

WHIT:

That's faith. It's the same way we put our faith in Jesus Christ. We trust Him, believing that He has—and *will*—do all that He said He would. The Bible says, "And though you have not seen Jesus, you love Him, and though you do not see Him now, but believe in Him, you greatly rejoice with joy inexpressible and full of glory, obtaining as a result of your faith, the salvation of your souls." That's 1 Peter 1:8 and 9.

LUCY:

Thanks for telling us, Mr. Whittaker. I'll remember that when they pick on me at school.

JACK:

But what happened to Noah?

WHIT:

Noah? He lived for another 350 years.

JACK:

Wow! That's . . . that's . . . (MUMBLING) Lessee, he was 600 years old when . . . and . . . 350 . . . (BRIGHTLY) He was 950 years old when he died!

WHIT:

Yep.

JACK:

Will *I* live to be 950 years old if I have the faith of Noah?

WHIT:

Jack, if you have faith like Noah, you'll live forever.

[MUSIC BRIDGE TAKES US TO . . . THE END. BLACKOUT OR CURTAIN.]

Over the Airwaves

INTRODUCTION

Over the Airwaves, originally aired on January 19, 1991, was another episode in the Kid's Radio format. This time we turned our attention to some of Jesus' parables about the kingdom of heaven in Matthew chapters 21 and 22. True to form, however, our stories aren't exact retellings of those parables, but offer a couple of twists on what Jesus was communicating.

PRODUCTION NOTES

Like *The Big Broadcast*, this is a sketch-based program that gives you flexibility with your production. You can do the entire script as a full-blown play or use only the sections that you want. This can be performed in a true "live" radio drama style, with microphones, music stands, and sound effects. Or a reader's theatre approach might work better. Or you may want to mix live performance with prerecorded sections or quick bits read from off-stage. It's up to you.

The set can be a "radio station" with microphones and sound effects scattered all over. The main announcer/narrator can read from a podium off to one side. You can take dramatic "license" and set up sections of the stage to accommodate the various scenes as simply or elaborately as you want. For example, the call-in with Connie can take place to the extreme left or right of the stage. As for "Young Guns Bonanza in the Big Valley," this is a chance to get everyone dressed up in cowboy outfits—and have fun!

The first scene and last section with Connie are optional.

CAST OF CHARACTERS

CONNIE: *intrepid teenager*

LUCY: *11- to 12-year-old girl*

WHIT: *our wise and wonderful mentor and* ANNOUNCER

EUGENE: *our brainy and trusty companion*

GEORGE BARCLAY: *a father*

DONNA BARCLAY: *a 13-year-old daughter*

JIMMY BARCLAY: *an 11-year-old son*

JESUS

CHIEF PRIEST

SECOND PRIEST

MATT CARTWOOD: *any variation on "Bonanza's" Ben Cartright, "The Big Valley's" Jarrod Barclay, or Andy Griffith*

WES CHESTER: *should be played as Walter Brennan or Dennis Weaver from his "Gunsmoke" days*

JEREMY CARTWOOD: *could be any combination of Heath Barclay ("The Big Valley"), Little Joe ("Bonanza"), or Patrick Wayne (John's son)*

HEADLOCK HARRY: *a mangy villain*

TRIGGER-FINGER TROY: *another mangy villain*

SILVER-SADDLESLAPPER STEPHANIE: *a mangy villain*

THE APOSTLE JOHN

THE CROWD: *extras*

SCENE 1
[WHIT'S END, A MEETING ROOM, ON A TUESDAY NIGHT. CONNIE IS THERE, SETTING UP A RADIO IN THE FRONT OF THE ROOM. SHE IS TRYING TO FIND THE APPROPRIATE RADIO STATION.]

CONNIE:
Hm. Now where is it?

[SHE FIDDLES SOME MORE UNTIL SHE HEARS WHAT SHE NEEDS TO HEAR.]

CONNIE:
Ah, this must be it.

[SHE TURNS THE RADIO DOWN SO WE HEAR IT SOFTLY IN THE BACKGROUND. LUCY ENTERS.]

LUCY:
(APPROACHING) Hi, Connie.

CONNIE:
Hello, Lucy. Bible study'll be ready to start in a minute.

LUCY:
Where is everybody?

CONNIE:
I don't know. Maybe they heard Whit was out of town for a few days and thought *I'd* be teaching.

LUCY:

I'm sure that isn't true.

CONNIE:

It doesn't matter. I'm not teaching anyway. Whit thought he'd try something new, since he couldn't be here in person. In fact, he was kinda nervous about whether it would work or not. Guess it doesn't matter since we're the only ones here.

LUCY:

Whether *what* would work?

CONNIE:

His new idea. We put it together last week.

LUCY:

What's his new idea?

CONNIE:

The radio.

LUCY:

The *radio?*

[MUSIC BRIDGE TAKES US STRAIGHT INTO WHIT'S RADIO BROADCAST.]

WHIT:

Whit's End presents Kid's Radio presenting (ECHO ON) "Adventures in the Bible"—(ECHO OFF) Bringing the *Bible* to life in *your* life!

[COMPLEMENTARY DRAMATIC MUSIC STING]

WHIT:

Tonight we're going to explore Matthew chapters 21 and 22 where Jesus told a few parables about the (ECHO ON) kingdom of heaven (ECHO OFF). In case you've forgotten, let's go to Eugene Meltsner for a brief yet simple definition of "parable." Eugene?

EUGENE:

Thank you, John Avery Whittaker. A parable is a narrative of imagined events used to illustrate a moral or spiritual lesson.

WHIT:

And now the English translation by Connie Kendall. Connie?

CONNIE:

A parable is a short, simple story that teaches a lesson.

WHIT:

Thanks, Connie. Matthew 21, beginning in verse 23, tells us that Jesus had performed several miracles among the people and, afterwards, entered the Temple courts. While He was teaching there, the chief priests and elders of the people came to Him.

[A CROWD HAS MOVED ONSTAGE, WITH JESUS AT THE CENTER.]

CHIEF PRIEST:

Tell us. By what authority are You doing these things?

WHIT:

—They asked.

SECOND PRIEST:

And *who* gave You this authority?

WHIT:

So Jesus replied:

JESUS:

I will ask you a question. If you answer Me, I will tell you by what authority I am doing these things. John the Baptist's baptism—did it come from heaven or from men?

WHIT:

The chief priests and elders discussed it among themselves and said . . .

[WE HEAR THE LOW MURMURING OF PEOPLE DISCUSSING SOMETHING AMONG THEMSELVES.]

CHIEF PRIEST:

(WHISPERING) If we answer "from heaven," then He'll ask us why we didn't believe John the Baptist.

SECOND PRIEST:

And if we answer "from men," then the people will hurt us because they thought John was a prophet!

WHIT:

So, they finally turned to Jesus and said:

PRIESTS AND ELDERS:

(SHRUGGING LIKE CHILDREN) We don't know.

WHIT:

And Jesus said:

JESUS:

Then I will not tell you by what authority I am doing what I do.

[AS THE CROWD MOVES ON, OUR ATTENTION MOVES TO ONE SIDE OF THE STAGE WITH CONNIE. SHE COULD BE SITTING AT A DESK OR STANDING AT A PODIUM. THERE SHOULD BE A PANEL OF SOME SORT IN FRONT OF HER SO SHE CAN "TAKE THE CALLS." THE CALLERS IN THIS SCENE CAN BE PERFORMED LIVE OFFSTAGE OR BE PRERECORDED FOR INCLUSION HERE.]

CONNIE:

This is "Call In to Connie," where we cap the questions from callers who care to call. Tonight's burning question: Who will get into the kingdom of heaven, based on Matthew 22 and 23? (HITS SWITCHBOARD BUTTON) You're on!

CALLER NO. 1:

Hi, Connie. I don't know what the Bible says, but I think the kingdom of heaven is inside all of us.

CONNIE:

Uh huh, that's a popular idea. But is it right? Next caller! (PUNCHES BUTTON)

CALLER NO. 2:

I think the kingdom of heaven is a product of the reincarnation of previous states of mind purified through crystals and proper dental hygiene.

CONNIE:

Whoops, bad connection. Next caller? (HITS BUTTON)

CALLER NO. 3:

Hi, Connie. Um, if I'm really, really, really good then I'll get into the kingdom of heaven.

CONNIE:

Thanks for calling. (PUNCHES BUTTON) And one last call . . .

CALLER NO. 4:

Maybe if I go to church?

CONNIE:

Maybe—and maybe not. Thank you for the calls to "Call In to Connie." Whit, what did those chapters in Matthew *really* tell us about the kingdom of heaven?

[CUT TO:]

WHIT:

Connie, the answer is found a series of parables Jesus told His listeners there. The first parable was about a father and his two children . . .

[THE BRIEFEST OF MUSIC STINGS; THE BARCLAY HOUSEHOLD; DONNA'S ROOM]

FATHER:

Donna.

DONNA:

Yeah, Dad?

FATHER:

I need you to mow the lawn this afternoon, OK?

DONNA:

Huh?

FATHER:

The lawn.

DONNA:

It's not my turn.

FATHER:

I don't know *whose* turn it is—just do it, OK?

DONNA:

But it's *Jimmy's* turn! Why can't *he* do it?

FATHER:
I didn't ask him. I just thought you—

DONNA:
I did it last week. It's Jimmy's turn.

FATHER:
All right, all right. I'll ask Jimmy.

[BRIEF MUSIC STING; THE LIVING ROOM; JIMMY IS WATCHING TELEVISION.]

FATHER:
Jimmy?

JIMMY:
Yeah, Dad?

FATHER:
Would you please mow the lawn? I understand
it's your turn.

JIMMY:
Sure, Dad. After the game is over, OK?

FATHER:
OK. Just so it doesn't go too late.

JIMMY:
It won't.

FATHER:
I have some errands to run. I'll be back in a little
while.

[BRIEF MUSIC STING. LATER. GEORGE ENTERS THE HOUSE AND THE LIVING ROOM
WHERE JIMMY IS WATCHING TV.]

FATHER:
(CALLING) Jimmy?

JIMMY:
Hi, Dad. Look, I'm sorry I didn't get the lawn
mowed, but this great movie came on, and I was
gonna do it as soon as it was over and—

FATHER:
But the lawn *is* mowed. I was just coming in to
thank you for doing such a good job.

JIMMY:

Oh . . . well, I didn't do it.

FATHER:

Then who did? Your mom's at the church this afternoon.

JIMMY:

I'm sure it wasn't . . .

FATHER:

(SURPRISED) Donna?

DONNA:

Yeah?

FATHER:

You mowed the lawn?

DONNA:

Uh huh. Didn't you ask me to?

FATHER:

Yes, but . . . you said no.

DONNA:

I changed my mind. Didn't you like it?

FATHER:

No . . . it was a good job. A *very* good job.

[BRIEF MUSIC STING TAKES US BACK TO WHIT. JESUS AND THE CROWD RETURN TO THE STAGE.]

WHIT:

Jesus asked the crowd,

JESUS:

Which of the two children did what the father wanted?

CROWD:

The first!

WHIT:

And they were right. Jesus then explained that even the worst sinners would get into heaven ahead of the people who thought they could get in simply because they were "good" or "religious."

JESUS:

For John the Baptist came to show you the way of righteousness and you did not believe, but the tax collectors and women of bad reputation did. And even after you saw *their* change, you still did not repent and believe.

WHIT:

So, you see, it's not a matter of being good or going to church—though those things are important. It's a matter of repenting and believing.

CROWD:

(AS IF THEY FINALLY GET IT.) Ahhh!

WHIT:

This message wasn't really new to the leaders of Israel, you know. For years, God had sent prophets to tell them, but the outcome was always the same—as we see in the next parable Jesus told— and we'll retell with a slight change of scenery . . .

[CUT TO MUSIC WITH A DISTINCTLY "WESTERN MOVIE/TV THEME" FEEL.]

ANNOUNCER:

And now . . . "Young Guns Bonanza in the Big Valley"!

[A HORSE WHINNIES AND THE MUSIC CONTINUES.]

ANNOUNCER:

Our story begins deep in the heart of the great West—on the South Spoon Ranch where its kind-hearted owner, Matt Cartwood, is talking with his sidekick Wes Chester.

[WE CUT TO THE STUDY IN THE MASSIVE SOUTH SPOON RANCH MANSION. WES CHESTER, BY THE WAY, SHOULD BE PLAYED AS WALTER BRENNAN OR DENNIS WEAVER FROM HIS "GUNSMOKE" DAYS. MATT COULD BE ANY VARIATION ON BEN CARTRIGHT, JARROD BARCLAY, OR ANDY GRIFFITH.]

MATT CARTWOOD:

Well, Wes, the South Spoon Ranch is completed. We have a sprawling mansion, land as far as any eye can see, and the most successful trade in cattle and sheep anywhere west of the Mississippi.

WES:

You don't have to tell me, Mr. Cartwood. I've been with you from the beginning—splittin' logs, pushin' soil, herdin' cattle, and shearing sheep, yessiree.

MATT CARTWOOD:

I know it, Wes. But it's time to move on to new pastures where the logs aren't split, the soil isn't pushed, the cattle haven't heard, and the sheep are sure to be unshorn. Somewhere over that next mountain, Wes.

WES:

I know that look in your eye, Mr. Cartwood. You've got that itch again.

MATT CARTWOOD:

No, Wes. The powder took care of that. I'm talking about something bigger.

WES:

You have a rash?

MATT CARTWOOD:

Worse, Wes. I want you to get everyone packed. We're moving to California!

[SOMETHING RESEMBLING THE "BEVERLY HILLBILLIES" THEME MIGHT BE APPRO-PRIATE HERE—AND SHOULD PLAY UNDER THE ANNOUNCER'S LINES.]

ANNOUNCER:

Matt and Wes packed up their families, got the wagon train ready, and were just about to head into the sunset when—

WES:

Mr. Cartwood, I know I only have a brain the size of a molecule on the hind leg of a flea, but shouldn't you entrust someone to take care of the South Spoon Ranch while you're gone? Seems a waste to leave all those split logs, pushed soil, herded cattle, and—

MATT CARTWOOD:

I've been thinking the same thing, Wes. And that's why I took out an ad in the *Big Valley Gazette* for some good workers to come in and run the place while we're building new lives in California. They should be here any moment now.

[WE HEAR A HORSE TROTTING UP OUTSIDE—A "WHOA"—AND THE SOUND OF A MAN IN BOOTS STRIDING ACROSS THE WOODEN FRONT PORCH AND THEN ON-STAGE.]

WES:

Maybe this is one of 'em now, yessiree!

[THE DOOR OPENS AND JEREMY CARTWOOD ENTERS. HE COULD BE ANY COMBI-NATION OF HEATH AND NICK BARCLAY, LITTLE JOE, OR PATRICK WAYNE (JOHN'S SON).]

JEREMY:

Hello, Father!

WES:

And maybe it isn't.

MATT CARTWOOD:

It's my beloved son, Jeremy! How goes it, Jerms?

JEREMY:

Fine, Father. Even better if you didn't call me "Jerms."

MATT CARTWOOD:

Where have you been all day? Saving the lives of some oppressed mineworkers, I wouldn't doubt.

JEREMY:

No, actually I was—

MATT CARTWOOD:

Thwarting yet another train robbery on the West-bank Railroad.

JEREMY:

Not really, I—

MATT CARTWOOD:

Chasing off another renegade band of cattle rustlers.

JEREMY:

No! I was at the North Fork of South Spoon wav-ing goodbye to Mom and my dear sisters.

MATT CARTWOOD:

Oh. They made arrangements for us in town, then.

JEREMY:

Uh huh. From South Spoon's North Fork, they're
going to the Golden Knife Hotel in Pan Creek
Gulch near Kettle Gorge.

WES:

They have a nice blue plate special there, I've
heard. Yep.

MATT CARTWOOD:

Enough with the kitchen utensils. As soon as our
new tenants get here, we'll join the rest of our
dearly departed family.

[EXACTLY AS BEFORE, WE HEAR A HORSE TROTTING UP OUTSIDE—A "WHOA"—
AND THE SOUND OF A MAN IN BOOTS STRIDING ACROSS THE WOODEN FRONT
PORCH.]

WES:

Maybe this is them there now!

[DOOR OPENS AND THREE MEN(?) OF DUBIOUS CHARACTER ENTER. AND, YES, IT'S
ENTIRELY INCONSISTENT WITH THE SOUND EFFECT.]

THE THREE TENANTS:

Hiya. We're your new tenants!

WES:

Good thing.

MATT CARTWOOD:

I'm glad you finally made it. I'm Matt Cartwood,
this is my son, Jeremy—

JEREMY:

Hello.

MATT CARTWOOD:

And this is Wes, my trusty sidekick.

WES:

Yessiree, yep, yep.

HEADLOCK HARRY:

I'm Headlock Harry, and these are my boys.

TRIGGER-FINGER TROY:

I'm Trigger-Finger Troy.

SILVER-SADDLE STEPHANIE:

(CLEARLY A GIRL) I'm Silver-SaddleSlapper
Stephanie.

WES:

(ASIDE) Signin' your names must be a real chore.

JEREMY:

Wait a minute. Silver-SaddleSlapper Stephanie is
a girl's name. You're a girl!

SILVER-SADDLE STEPHANIE:

I am not.

JEREMY:

You are too.

SILVER-SADDLE STEPHANIE:

I am not. (QUICK DRAW, GUNS COCKED) And
I have two six-shooters that agree with me. Any
questions?

JEREMY:

Yeah. (BACKING DOWN) What's a nice lookin'
guy like you doin' in a place like this?

HEADLOCK HARRY:

Enough with this gibber-jabber! Are you leasing
the place to us or not?

MATT CARTWOOD:

Well . . . I had hoped a few more people would
answer the ad.

TRIGGER-FINGER TROY:

Maybe they were busy.

HEADLOCK HARRY:

(KNOWINGLY) Maybe they met with unfortu-
nate accidents on the way.

SILVER-SADDLE STEPHANIE:

Maybe they were waiting for the man from the
cable company to come.

MATT CARTWOOD:

(UNEASILY) Well . . . let's get the paperwork
filled out, and the South Spoon Ranch will be
yours to take care of.

HEADLOCK HARRY:
(OMINOUSLY) Oh—we'll take care of it all right.
(LOW LAUGH)

ANNOUNCER:
The Cartwoods left for—

WES:
And Wes.

ANNOUNCER:
The Cartwoods *and Wes* left for California where they split logs, pushed soil, herded cattle, and sheared sheep.

WES:
Yessiree!

ANNOUNCER:
But all was not well at the South Spoon Ranch.

[CUT TO MATT CARTWOOD AND WES IN THE STUDY AT THE LA QUINTA PIÑATA RANCH IN SOUTHERN CALIFORNIA.]

MATT CARTWOOD:
Wes, things are not well at the South Spoon Ranch.

WES:
So I've heard.

MATT CARTWOOD:
I've sent cables, letters, Hallmark cards, and even a picture of me with a rude look on my face. Our tenants won't answer or send me the money they owe us. What should we do?

WES:
I've already done it.

MATT CARTWOOD:
Done what?

WES:
Sent one of the ranch hands to go get your money. In fact, he should be back any minute now.

[WE HEAR A HORSE TROTTING UP OUTSIDE—A "WHOA"—AND THE SOUND OF A MAN IN BOOTS STRIDING ACROSS THE WOODEN FRONT PORCH.]

WES:

Maybe this is him now, yessiree!

[THE DOOR OPENS AND JEREMY CARTWOOD ENTERS.]

JEREMY:

Hello, Father!

WES:

And maybe it isn't.

MATT CARTWOOD:

It's my beloved son, Jeremy! How goes it, Jerms—er, *Son?*

JEREMY:

(SERIOUSLY) Father, the messenger Wes sent to the South Spoon Ranch has returned.

MATT CARTWOOD:

And?

JEREMY:

And our tenants grabbed him, beat him severely, and sent him home empty-handed.

MATT CARTWOOD:

Those scoundrels!

WES:

I don't reckon it's ever good policy to trust people who put violent idioms in front of their first names.

MATT CARTWOOD:

Where is the messenger now?

JEREMY:

In the ranch house. They're dressing his wounds.

WES:

(THROWAWAY) Hm. Must be usin' ranch house dressing.

JEREMY:

I think I should go talk to our tenants, Father.

MATT CARTWOOD:

No, Son, no. Let's send another man. Someone a little bigger, perhaps. Big John McBear should be able to reason with them.

[MUSIC AS THE ANNOUNCER SPEAKS]

ANNOUNCER:

So Big John McBear was sent—and returned empty-handed.

[THE STUDY—MATT CARTWOOD AND BIG JOHN McBEAR, WHO IS STANDING THERE WITH A BIG BANDAGE AROUND HIS HEAD]

MATT CARTWOOD:

Well, Big John, you went back to the South Spoon Ranch, spoke to Headlock, Trigger-Finger, and Silver-SaddleSlapper. What happened?

BIG JOHN McBEAR:

(WITH A BIG, BEAR-LIKE VOICE—BUT WHIN-ING LIKE A LITTLE BOY) They called me names, then hit me in the head!

MATT CARTWOOD:

That does it. Wes!

WES:

(ENTERS) Yessiree, yep?

MATT CARTWOOD:

Send Confrontational Conrad. He'll persuade them to pay.

WES:

Yessiree.

[MUSIC UNDERSCORE]

ANNOUNCER:

Confrontational Conrad went to the South Spoon Ranch and encountered a different fate than the previous messengers.

[A JOLT OF DRAMATIC MUSIC; IN THE STUDY WITH MATT AND WES]

MATT CARTWOOD:

Say that again, Wes.

WES:

They killed Confrontational Conrad.

MATT CARTWOOD:

I don't understand their behavior, Wes. We signed a contract! We agreed in good faith! We even sang songs around a campfire together! *We had a relationship*!

WES:

What do you reckon we should do, Mr. Cartwood?

MATT CARTWOOD:

Send a *gang* of men. Maybe a collection of gun-toting, seasoned cowboys with large biceps and craggy faces will show them I'm serious about this!

WES:

Yessiree!

MATT CARTWOOD:

And, Wes—

WES:

Huh?

MATT CARTWOOD:

I want *you* to lead them.

WES:

I had a feeling you were going to say that.

[MUSICAL UNDERSCORE]

ANNOUNCER:

Wes and the gang went to the South Spoon Ranch, but you can guess what happened.

[WE HEAR FROM OFFSTAGE WHAT INITIALLY SOUNDS LIKE A GUNFIGHT, BUT IT HAS A THIN, ALMOST TELEVISION SOUND TO IT. WHICH IS APPROPRIATE, SINCE IT IS A TELEVISION. IT CONTINUES EVEN AS MATT CARTWOOD TALKS OFFSTAGE.]

MATT CARTWOOD:

Wes?

WES:

Huh?

MATT CARTWOOD:

Turn off the TV, will you?

WES:

Oh.

[HE CLICKS THE REMOTE AND THE TV TURNS OFF.]

MATT CARTWOOD:

Thank you. Come into the study; I want to talk to you.

[THEY WALK ONTO THE STAGE. WES IS COVERED WITH BANDAGES. HE SPEAKS AS THEY ENTER.]

WES:

Watchin' TV is all a wounded, bandaged man has to do around here during the day. Never liked soap operas.

MATT CARTWOOD:

Wes, you've had time to recover. I think you better tell me what happened.

WES:

This fella named Rocky from Dakota went into a saloon to meet up with a girl named McGill or Lil, but everyone knew her as Nancy—

MATT CARTWOOD:

Not on TV. I meant at the South Spoon Ranch.

WES:

Well, sir, it was terrible. A massacre. They called us names and pushed us around and beat us up and shot at us and sent the whole gang running and . . . frankly, I don't want to talk about it.

MATT CARTWOOD:

I understand. I don't know what's left for me to do. I'm not a man of violence. I don't believe it ever solves anything. There must be someone I could send to the South Spoon Ranch that they would *have* to respect. But who?

[DOOR OPENS—JEREMY STRIDES IN.]

JEREMY:

Hello, Father. Hiya, Wes. How're you feeling?

WES:

Just dandy for a man who's been called names, beat up, shot at, and sent running. But I'd rather not talk about it.

JEREMY:

I understand.

MATT CARTWOOD:

Jeremy?

JEREMY:

Yes, Father?

MATT CARTWOOD:

There's something I need you to do.

[DRAMATIC MUSIC BRIDGE]

SCENE 2
[MUSIC UP]

ANNOUNCER:

Believing that Headlock Harry, Trigger-Finger Troy, and Silver-SaddleSlapper Stephanie would respect his son, Matt Cartwood sent Jeremy to the South Spoon Ranch to collect the overdue rent.

[OUTSIDE OF THE SOUTH SPOON RANCH]

HEADLOCK HARRY:

Well, Silver-SaddleSlapper Stephanie, this is workin' out a whole lot better than I coulda planned. We got the South Spoon Ranch, and Matt Cartwood can't do a thing about it.

SILVER-SADDLE STEPHANIE:

He could send more men, Headlock Harry.

HEADLOCK HARRY:

(LAUGHS VICIOUSLY) He's probably run out of men by now.

[TRIGGER-FINGER TROY ENTERS.]

TRIGGER-FINGER TROY:
(BREATHLESSLY) Headlock! Silver-SaddleSlap-per! You'll never guess who just checked in to the Golden Knife Hotel!

HEADLOCK HARRY:
Who?

TRIGGER-FINGER TROY:
You have to guess.

HEADLOCK HARRY:
(ANNOYED) Trigger-Finger!

TRIGGER-FINGER TROY:
No. Guess again.

SILVER-SADDLE STEPHANIE:
The Cavalry's fifth legion regiment from the Pon-derosa Valley?

TRIGGER-FINGER TROY:
No. But you're gettin' close.

HEADLOCK HARRY:
Who, Trigger-Finger?

TRIGGER-FINGER TROY:
If you're gonna get nasty about it, I don't think I'm gonna tell you.

HEADLOCK HARRY:
Troy—tell me right now or I'll blab your *real* name to everyone in town.

TRIGGER-FINGER TROY:
You wouldn't.

HEADLOCK HARRY:
Try me.

TRIGGER-FINGER TROY:
(PAUSE, GIVES IN) All right. Jeremy Cartwood just checked in, that's who.

HEADLOCK HARRY:
The son! Perfect!

SILVER-SADDLE STEPHANIE:

Perfect? But . . . he's the *son*. We'll *have to* give 'em the rent now.

HEADLOCK HARRY:

Not a chance, Silver-SaddleSlapper Stephanie. He's Matt Cartwood's heir. If we get rid of him, the South Spoon Ranch could be ours to *own*! Trigger-Finger!

TRIGGER-FINGER TROY:

What?

HEADLOCK HARRY:

Take a message to Mister Jeremy Cartwood.

TRIGGER-FINGER TROY:

Right! See you later!

[TRIGGER-FINGER EXITS, AND WE HEAR HIM GET ON THE HORSE AND RIDE OFF. SILENCE FOR A MOMENT, THEN WE HEAR HIM APPROACHING AGAIN. HE GETS OFF HIS HORSE AND ENTERS AGAIN.]

TRIGGER-FINGER TROY:

What message, Headlock Harry?

HEADLOCK HARRY:

Tell him to meet us at the North Fork of South Spoon at *high noon*. We wanna have a little talk at him—with *lead*. (LAUGHS VICIOUSLY) Any questions?

SILVER-SADDLE STEPHANIE:

Just one. What *is* your real name, Trigger-Finger? I've been a member of this gang for years, and I don't know.

HEADLOCK HARRY:

Tell her, Troy.

TRIGGER-FINGER TROY:

Aw, do I hafta?

HEADLOCK HARRY:

Tell her.

TRIGGER-FINGER TROY:

It's . . . it's Stubbyfingers Stanley.

SILVER-SADDLE STEPHANIE:
(CONSIDERING IT) That's not so bad. *My* real name is FishFace Francine.

[BRIEF MUSIC BRIDGE AS THE ANNOUNCER SPEAKS]

ANNOUNCER:
Stubbyfingers Stanley went to—

TRIGGER-FINGER TROY:
(THREATENING, TO THE ANNOUNCER) Trigger-Finger Troy to *you*, bub.

ANNOUNCER:
Trigger-Finger Troy went to town with the message.

[A HALLWAY AT THE GOLDEN KNIFE HOTEL. TRIGGER-FINGER KNOCKS ON JEREMY CARTWOOD'S DOOR. HE OPENS IT.]

JEREMY:
Yes?

TRIGGER-FINGER TROY:
Jeremy Cartwood, I'm Stub—er, Trigger-Finger Troy from the South Spoon Ranch.

JEREMY:
Yes, I remember you. Have you come with the overdue rent?

TRIGGER-FINGER TROY:
No. Just this: meet us at the North Fork of South Spoon at high noon.

JEREMY:
I'm a man of peace, Trigger-Finger. I don't want any trouble. My father has been more than patient. We just want what you agreed to pay us for living on the South Spoon.

TRIGGER-FINGER TROY:
Don't you worry, Boy. Just be at the North Fork at high noon and you'll get what's coming to you.

JEREMY:
Then I'll be there.

[DOOR CLOSES—TRIGGER-FINGER EXITS. MUSICAL UNDERSCORE WITH AN-
NOUNCER.]

ANNOUNCER:
High noon at the North Fork of South Spoon!

[BURST OF MUSIC—SOMETHING BIG AND DRAMATIC WOULD BE NICE; WE THEN
HEAR JEREMY RIDE UP ON HIS HORSE . . .]

JEREMY:
Whoa there, Bethesda!

[HORSE STOPS, AND HE CLIMBS OFF AND ENTERS THE STAGE.]

JEREMY:
Look at this place. It seems like—oh—20 minutes
ago that I stood on this spot and waved goodbye
to my beloved mother and treasured sisters.

HEADLOCK HARRY:
(FROM A DISTANCE) Cartwood! Jeremy Cartwood!

JEREMY:
Who is that? (CALLING BACK) I'm here! To
whom am I speaking?

[OUR THREE VILLAINS ARE OFFSTAGE, SURROUNDING JEREMY.]

HEADLOCK HARRY:
Headlock Harry!

TRIGGER-FINGER TROY:
And Trigger-Finger Troy!

SILVER-SADDLE STEPHANIE:
And Silver-SaddleSlapper Stephanie!

JEREMY:
I'm glad you all could make it. Why don't you
come this way, and we'll settle our accounts?

HEADLOCK HARRY:
No—*we'll* settle the accounts, Cartwood! Draw
your gun!

JEREMY:
No! This is no way to settle a dispute!

HEADLOCK HARRY:
Draw your gun! I'm gonna count to three.

JEREMY:
I won't do it!

HEADLOCK HARRY:
One!

JEREMY:
You don't know what you're doing.

TRIGGER-FINGER TROY:
Two!

JEREMY:
You'll spill innocent blood!

SILVER-SADDLE STEPHANIE:
Three!

HEADLOCK HARRY:
Now *draw!*

JEREMY:
Father!

[HIS SHOUT ECHOES—VERY LITERALLY—INTO A BLACKOUT. THERE IS NUMB SI-
LENCE FOR A MOMENT—DEAD AIR. JESUS AND THE CROWD SLOWLY RETURN TO
THE STAGE.]

WHIT:
Then Jesus turned to the crowd and asked:

JESUS:
What will the owner do? He will come and kill
those tenants and give the property to others.

WHIT:
When the people heard this, they said:

CROWD:
No! May this never be!

WHIT:
Jesus said to them:

84

JESUS:

Haven't you read the Scriptures? "The stone the builders rejected has become the cornerstone; the Lord has done this, and it is marvelous in our eyes."

WHIT:

Jesus was quoting Psalm 118, then explained:

JESUS:

Therefore I tell you that the kingdom of God will be taken away from you and given to a people who will produce its fruit. He who falls on this stone will be broken to pieces, but whoever it falls on will be crushed.

WHIT:

And do you think the chief priests were impressed? Do you think they realized how wrong they had been? Do you imagine that they stopped for a moment, considered repenting, and accepted Jesus as their Savior? (PAUSE) The Book of Matthew goes on to tell us that when the chief priests and Pharisees heard Jesus' parables, they knew He was talking about them. Then they began to look for a way to arrest Him—to have Him put to death. Later, they did. And, in that way, the parable Jesus told actually came true. (BEAT) The apostle John—a close disciple of Jesus— would later write:

JOHN:

(STEPS ONSTAGE) He was in the world, and though the world was made through Him, the world did not recognize Him. He came to those who were His own, but His own did not receive Him. Yet, to all who received Him, to those who believed in His name, He gave the right to become children of God.

WHIT:

(PAUSE) I hope you've enjoyed this rather different approach to our usual Bible study time together. Thank you for listening. This is John Avery Whittaker for "Adventures in the Bible" from Kid's Radio.

[WE HEAR SOMETHING RESEMBLING A DRAMATIC THEME BEGIN TO PLAY—BUT

GETS CUT OFF WHEN CONNIE TURNS THE RADIO OFF.]

CONNIE:

Well, that's it for our Bible study tonight. Whit wanted me to find out if you liked it or not. What did you think, Lucy?

LUCY:

I liked it.

CONNIE:

And how about the rest of you?

[WE HEAR A LARGE CROWD OF KIDS CHEERING EXUBERANTLY.]

CONNIE:

(OVER THE APPLAUSE, GIGGLES) I'll be sure to tell him.

[MUSIC RISES AND TAKES US TO . . . THE END.]